THE
PRE-LAW SUMMER SCHOOL
WRITING GUIDE

THE
PRE-LAW SUMMER SCHOOL
WRITING GUIDE

ANGEL EVERETT, ESQ.

Paperback ISBN-13: 978-0-9990641-1-5

Table of Contents

PART C: Tricks Of The Trade

INTRODUCTION

◇◇◇◇◇

HOW TO USE THIS BOOK

Although *Harvard and Hardship: A Beginner's Guide to College and Law School* includes some basic insights into analytical writing, there is so much more instruction to be given about how to produce a quality research paper.

But there is no need to fear. All too often I hear the Imposter Syndrome-induced saying, "I am not a good writer," as if that diagnosis of one's writing skills is a fin al verdict, as opposed to an opportunity to be taught how to write. Honestly, writing is simple, especially analytical writing. If you think you're "just not a good writer," I'd like to challenge your thinking pattern: Perhaps it's not that you're not a good writer, but that no one has taught you a writing formula. If you can think, you can write. If you can hold a conversation, you can write. If you have an opinion about something, you can write. If you can comment on the latest celebrity gossip, you can write.

The purpose of this writing guide is to annihilate the myth that analytical writing is so inherently difficult that only a few, pre-selected "wise ones" can do it. Writing. Is. S imple. Yes, it takes time, planning, and discipline, as you must force yourself to sit down and get your ideas out, but the formula is simple.

This writing guide is intended to be a reference resource, meaning that when you sit down to start researching or writing, you will have this book right there with you, metaphorically holding your hand as you write your paper. Do not read this book straight through, from beginning to end. Do not try to memorize everything mentioned. Instead, use the Table of Contents to select the chapter that fits your writing needs in the moment. As you write more and more papers, you'll start to remember the diffe rent structures and tips provided herein, and eventually you'll be able write independently.

As a final note: the enclosed suggestions will provide structure and help ease anxiety, fear, and frustration about how to approach your research papers. Ultimately, however, it will be **your** focus, **your** discipline, **your** consistency, and **your** hard work that will achieve the grade you are hoping to make. (Which, I hope, is an A+ ;-)

I wish you all the best in your educational goals, and remember, smartness can be achieved. You are smart!

Angel Everett, Esq.

Founder/CEO, Angel the Law School Coach LLC

PART A

Research Papers

What distinguishes college and graduate school writing from the reports you may have written in elementary and/or middle school?

Analysis

Basic reports are simply a regurgitation of facts. For instance, common report assignments require you to collect a bunch of information about a place, person, or whatever topic the teacher has chosen, then report back to the classroom. That reporting could be in the form of a written report, or perhaps even an oral report (i.e., a presentation accompanied by a PowerPoint or a poster). Either way, in the sum of things, the student is being asked to gather information, summarize it, and then spew it back to the teacher or to her peers.

On the other hand, college and university-level writing takes it up a notch because the expectation is that not only will the student gather and summarize the information, but she will also ***do something*** with it. That she will analyze it. Now, don't let that word, "analyze" or "analytical paper" or "write an analysis" scare you. It's just a fancy word telling you ***do something*** with the information you have gathered:

First, dissect it. Break it apart. Examine the different parts, viewpoints, opinions, causes, and effects.

Second, do any one (or all, if space permits) of the following with the various parts:

- Comment.
- Disagree.

- Share your opinion.
- Share your experience.
- Compare something you found with something else you gathered.
- Contrast the information you gathered against something you already know.
- Compare similar perspectives. Contrast the different ones.

It doesn't matter! As long as you ***dissect*** the topic and ***do something*** with the information you've gathered, *Tah-Dah!* You've written a college-level analytical paper.

This guide provides two formulas for college analytical writing. I successfully used either of these two writing formulas in college (and when applicable, in law school) every time I was tasked with writing a research paper.

1) The Quote and Comment – Use this approach to answer a particular research question.
2) The Observe and Cite – Use this approach when you know what observation you want to make, or you know what point you want to prove.

> If you are having difficulty choosing between the *Quote and Comment* and the *Observe and Cite*, it is fine to arbitrarily choose one. Choosing a writing framework should not be a source of confusion or frustration. Just choose one writing method, and use the pertinent chapter as a guide to get to work. It will come together in the end.

Chapter 1

The Quote and Comment Method

Use the Quote and Comment approach when you are using your paper to: 1) answer particular research questions, or 2) learn about a specific subject. As you complete the research and draft your writing plan, the answer(s) to your research question will become clear.

The Quote and Comment Formula

1) Gather your sources.

- Begin your research by gathering books, journal articles, opinion pieces, and news articles on the topic. All such research materials can be found in the library. If you are unsure how to use your library's catalog system, ask the librarian to teach you how to find books (or articles, etc.) on the topic. Most librarians love to help.
- Do not overwhelm yourself by gathering too many books or articles. The number of sources you need totally depends on the length of your research paper, but as a general rule of thumb, I usually aimed to leave the library with a five to eight research sources (i.e., books, journal articles, opinion pieces, etc.) If you need more, you can always return to the library and/or research online.
- Start early. I was never an *all-nighter* student. For me, that produced too much anxiety and stress. Hence, I suggest beginning this phase of your paper a couple of

weeks before the paper is due. (For instance, for a five- to ten-page paper, I believe the research phase should begin at least **two to three weeks** before the paper is due.) That way, if you don't find anything of interest at first, you have plenty of time to take another trip to the library to find what you need.

2) Go on a reading hunt.

- Now it is time to go digging through all those books, articles, etc. that you gathered to find the information you need. Do not be intimated by the thickness of the books or the length of the articles. After all, you are not reading these sources leisurely, like you would read a fictional novel or a comic book, but instead, you are a reader on a mission. **You are reading to pull out specific information for your paper:** Pick up a book, and glance at the chapter titles. Hop to the chapter that you think is most pertinent to your paper. Then as you read the chapter, keep in mind that your eyes are like laser radars on a special assignment to detect information that you can take back to your research paper and comment on. The same goes for reading journal articles or any other source: you are reading with focus, as you are on a mission to find information to later comment on in your paper.

- As you read, highlight (or otherwise take note of) those quotes, paragraphs, and research findings that you found interesting, or that you want to comment on in your research paper. Practically speaking, this step may be a list of quotes, paragraphs, and research findings that are typed, verbatim from the source, into a Microsoft Word document. Be sure to label each quote, paragraph, or research finding with the source and page number. That way, citations (to be discussed in Chapter 6) are a breeze.

3) Comment on the information you have chosen to highlight.

This is where the analytical writing begins. Again, analysis is just a fancy word for interacting with and/or responding to the information you have gathered. Take one quote, paragraph, or research finding at a time (from the list generated above in Step 2), and plan how you want to respond to it.

Here are some ideas:

- Your opinion about the fact you found.
- How one quote reminds you of something else.
- Was a research finding surprising to you?
- Compare two different quotes you found.
- Contrast two different pieces of information or opinions you found.

- Explain how your opinion changed based on something you read.
- The ideas are limitless. Respond, in your own way, to the information you have gathered.

4) Make a plan (also known as a "working outline").

Before you begin to write, you must plan. Planning makes writing easier. Planning gives form, structure, and purpose to your paper, making it a well-written, quality product, as opposed to random rambling you've transcribed just to meet a word count. Trust me, professors can tell the difference, and they are more likely to appreciate (and therefore assign a better grade to) a well-written, thought-out final product than some random sentences and ideas that have been mindlessly pieced together. See page 6 for an example plan for a Quote and Comment paper.

5) Write your research paper.

Using your plan as a guide, write by adding more "meat" (i.e. substance) to your plan.

- Specifically, actually explain the ideas you listed in your plan.
- Where ever your plan says, "Give opinion on X," write details that show what your opinion is and why it is so.
- Compare the things you promised to compare.
- Wherever your plan says, *contrast*, make sure you insert a paragraph that explains the differences between the two things you promised in your plan to contrast.
- Continue so on and so forth, until you have checked off everything on your plan.

The Quote And Comment Plan

The plan for a Quote and Comment paper is simply a list of all the research you highlighted as interesting (i.e., the quotes, facts, research findings, etc. from the "reading hunt" in Step 2), embedded with how you want to respond to each piece of information:

I. Quote, Fact, or Research Finding #1 (Source)
  *Commentary

II. Quote, Fact, or Research Finding #2 (Source)
  *Commentary

III. Quote, Fact, or Research Finding #3 (Source)
  *Commentary

Add as many quotes, facts, or findings (using Roman numerals) as necessary to meet the minimum word count or page limit. Also, add as many commentaries (*asterisks) as you would like under each quote, fact, or finding. Once your plan is completed, you are ready to begin writing your research paper.

Example Of A Quote And Comment Plan/Working Outline

◇◇◇◇◇◇◇◇

Topic: The Best Theme Parks

I. Introduction

II. Quote: "Disney parks in the United States and Japan held seven of the top 10 spots... Universal Studios came in second place with three parks in the top 10 list..." (Source: Article, CNN Travel. "World's 25 Most Popular Amusement Parks," July 4, 2017.)

Commentary: Speculate why Disney parks rank so highly.

Commentary: Comment on how it's surprising that Japan theme parks are ranked highly as well. Speculate why? (Maybe because of the high population of nearby Asian countries?)

Commentary: Compare my personal experience at Disney vs. Universal

III. Fact: There are 12 Disney theme parks in the world. (Source: Fake Journal Article, Volume 1,000, p. 2,000.)

Commentary: Compare this to the number of Six Flags theme parks in the world.

Commentary: Provide my opinion on why there are so many Disney theme parks.

IV. Research Finding: Walt Disney is known to have investigated park-goers to learn how many steps they took before dropping trash on the ground. That way, he would know how frequently to place garbage cans throughout the park. (Source: Fake Theme park Encyclopedia. Volume 0, page 0.)

Commentary: I think this was brilliant planning. Explain my opinion.

Commentary: Explain what other investigations I would do if I were building a theme park: What music to play and frequency of bathroom locations. Also, explain how I would conduct my investigations.

V. Conclusion

CHAPTER 2

THE OBSERVE AND CITE METHOD

Use the Observe and Cite Method when you want to make an observation about the world, people, a place, etc. In other words, this formula comes handy when you already have an opinion, idea, or point you want to prove, and you want your research paper to help you prove that point:

> The sky is blue.
>
> Fingerprints are unreliable.
>
> Most people don't care about politics.

Whatever the case may be, the Observe and Cite Method will help you structure your observations and research.

THE OBSERVE AND CITE FORMULA

1) Brainstorm your observation.

Write down the point you want to prove, as well as different variations of it. Brainstorming the point(s) you want to prove will help you narrow down your paper topic (and therefore make your research much easier). Example:

The sky is blue.

The sky is blue most of the time.

The sky is never purple.

Most people believe the sky is blue.

Depending on the complexity of your paper, you may have more than one observation to make or point to prove. In that case, complete a separate brainstorming list for each observation/point in your paper. Again, the purpose of this step is simply to flush out your ideas, so you have clarity on your paper topic and are able to focus your research.

EXAMPLE

Observation #1

The sky is blue.

The sky is never purple.

Most people believe the sky is blue.

Observation #2

Grass is green.

Grass is never neon.

Healthy grass is green.

Once you are done brainstorming, choose the final observation(s) that will serve as the topic of your research paper.

2) Gather your sources.

- Head to the library, or log on to an online database, to find books, journal articles, newspaper articles, or research papers on the topic. If you have many observations to make in your paper, you will want to find a source for each observation. However, be careful not to overwhelm yourself by trying to find a source for *every* minute fact or statement you make. This step is mainly for finding sources for the **major observations** that are the purpose, the backbone of your research paper.

- Note that the source(s) may support your observation, but it may not re-state your observation verbatim. However, even if the source doesn't support your observation directly, still hold on to that source. You may be able to make use of it in your paper. For instance, the source may support your observation by giving a similar opinion, providing context, or giving some historical background about the subject. If so, you can use that source to add more dimension and analysis to your paper. Or, the source may even contradict your observation or point you want to prove. Still hold on to it. Chapter 3, "The However Paragraph," shows how to use such contrary information to your advantage.

- Do not overwhelm yourself by gathering too many books or articles. As a general rule of thumb, for an Observe and Cite paper, I usually aim for one to three sources (i.e., books, journal articles, opinion pieces, etc.) for each major observation. If you need more sources, you can always return to the library.

- Start early! For me, waiting until the last minute to complete a term paper resulted in anxiety and stress. Hence, I suggest beginning this phase of your paper a couple of weeks before the paper is due. (For instance, for a five to ten-page paper that is following the Observe and Cite method, I believe the research phase should begin at least **three weeks** before the paper is due.) That way, if you can't find a source to support your observation(s), you have plenty of time to take another trip to the library to find what you need or to change what observation(s) you want to make.

3) Go on a reading hunt.

- Read the sources you have gathered with laser-beam eyes. You are on a mission to detect sentences, graphs, opinions, and facts that support – or at least comment on – your observation.

- As you read, take note of those sentences, graphs, opinions, etc. that are pertinent to your observation. Also, be sure to write down the title of the source and page number (i.e., write the citation). Remember, this method is called the Observe ***and Cite***. Take note of the citation now. That way, you won't have to painstakingly go back and flip through all those books and journals, trying to find where a piece of information came from.

> Remember, if you get lost as you look for sources, ask the librarian for help.

- Again, even if you come across information that disagrees with, or is the opposite of the point you are trying to prove, don't toss it out. You may be able to use that information in a "However Paragraph." (See Chapter 3, "The However Paragraph")

4) Make a plan. (Write your working outline.)

To avoid digressing into the dark abyss of theory and superfluous words, create a writing plan. Professors can tell the difference between a well-thought-out final product and some random sentences mindlessly pieced together, and they are more likely to assign a better grade to the former. Below is a template to help get you started.

THE OBSERVE AND CITE PLAN

◇◇◇◇◇◇◇

I. State observation #1

***Cite** to a source that supports, provides context, or disagrees with observation #1

-Add commentary

***Cite** to a source that supports, provides context, or disagrees with observation #1

-Add commentary

II. State observation #2

***Cite** to a source that supports, provides context, or disagrees with observation #2

-Add commentary

***Cite** to a source that supports, provides context, or disagrees with observation #2

-Add commentary

Add as many observations as necessary to prove your point, or to meet the minimum word count or page limit. Also, for each observation, add as many sources and commentaries as is necessary to explain and analyze your observation. Once your plan is completed, you are ready to begin writing your research paper.

5) Write your Observe and Cite research paper.

Add meat to your paper via your "commentary." Here are some suggestions for commentary:

* Thoroughly explain your observation(s) in your own words.

* Flush out your ideas by giving the 5W's of each idea:

  - What is your idea/opinion/observation?
  - Why do you hold that belief?
  - Who else believes similarly? (A particular researcher? Author? Political analyst? Professor? A specific cultural group?)
  - Where else is this idea prominent? (In a certain culture? In certain parts of the country?)
  - When was this idea first conceived?
  - When did you think of it?
  - Is it something people have thought for centuries, or has it gained popularity only recently? Explain all sides of the argument. Explain other perspectives.
  - How was this idea formed? How did you come to make this observation?

* Compare and/or contrast your observations with the observations or opinions of another author, researcher, professional, or institution.

* Compare (and/or contrast) two sources.

* Provide your opinion.

* Elaborate on your personal experience.

Also, note that it is not always necessary to include a direct quote from the source. In fact, doing so can get boring for the reader and make your writing sound too choppy and formulaic. Try mixing in direct-quotes with paraphrased information.

Example Of An Observe And Cite Plan

Topic: Nature is Colorful

I. Introduction

II. Observation: The sky is blue.

* **Cite:** "The sky is blue due to air molecules that scatter blue light away from the sun. Blue is scattered more than other colors because it travels in smaller waves." (Weather Encyclopedia Vol. 0, p. 0:)

- Add commentary about your observation or the cited source.

- Add commentary about your observation or the cited source.

III. Observation: Grass is green.

* **Cite:** "Grass is a plant, and so, therefore, it produces a pigment called chlorophyll. Chlorophyll is bright and mostly reflects the color green." (Fake Science Article, p. 1,000)

- Add commentary about your observation or the cited source.

- Add commentary about your observation or the cited source.

IV. Observation: Animals are colorful.

* **Cite**: "Geckos range in color from red, orange, green, to shades of brown or grey." (Animal Encyclopedia Vol 0, p. 0)

- Add commentary about your observation or the cited source.

* **Cite:** "Most leopards are tan to brown, with dark brown and black spots. However, in some cases, leopards are white with black spots." (Faux Animal Source, p. 0)

-Add commentary about your observation or the cited source.

* **Cite:** "There are over 9,000 species of birds, and they come in different color combinations." (The Bird Bible, p. 0)

-Add commentary about your observation or the cited source.

V. Conclusion

CHAPTER 3

THE HOWEVER PARAGRAPH

The However Paragraph is a useful tool to turn a dull, boring paper into an advanced, analytical paper. Basically, after you make a point in your research paper, you can throw in a However Paragraph that provides an alternative viewpoint. Doing so will probably get you extra brownie points (which, hopefully, convert to real points and a higher grade ;-).

Why? Think about it like this: to analyze something means to pick it apart, or to give it a detailed examination. So, adding a However Paragraph is a fool-proof way to add analytical complexity to your research paper because it demonstrates that you have taken the time to pick apart the topic or opinion. It shows the professor that you have considered multiple perspectives, and that you will respond to all facets of the issue. See? Easy-peasy.

FORMULA FOR THE HOWEVER PARAGRAPH

1) Review your plan.

- Whether you are writing a Quote and Comment paper, an Observe and Cite paper, or have come up with your own structure, you must plan. I must say that I agree with the axiom: "If you fail to plan, you plan to fail."

- Next, look for areas where you can offer a different perspective. For instance, you may have come across this different perspective when you were gathering and reviewing materials during the research phase. Or, you may just know of a different perspective by common knowledge, something you read a while back, or something you saw on the news. Either way, use your knowledge (be it recently-learned or something you just know) to offer an alternative viewpoint in the However Paragraph.

2) Plug in However Paragraphs.

- Wherever you have provided an opinion, a commentary, or a debatable research finding, write a note in your plan to add a However Paragraph.
- Also, jot down a sentence or two (as well as the citation source, if applicable), reminding yourself what the alternative viewpoint is that you will introduce in that However Paragraph.
- Note: Instead of inserting a However Paragraph after an opinion or commentary within your paper, it may also be an effective analytical strategy to insert a However Paragraph at the end of your paper to provide an entirely different viewpoint on the overall thesis, or observation, of your paper. I know what you're thinking: *But Angel, why would I do that?* Doesn't that weaken my argument? No! It can actually strengthen your analysis. Again, the However Paragraph shows that you are not closeminded to one idea, but that you have considered many viewpoints. Think about it like this: When you write your paper, the ball is in your court. Inserting a However Paragraph at the end of your paper allows you to bring in the counterargument on your own terms. That way, you can respond to the However Paragraph by adding a rebuttal-response (after the However Paragraph).

How to Begin a However Paragraph: Cue Words

◇◇◇◇◇◇◇

Obviously, you should begin a However Paragraph with the word, "However," as it alerts the professor that you are about to offer a counter-argument or contrasting research finding. But, if you have already used the word, "however" too many times in your paper, here are some alternative words and phrases to use in its place:

Interestingly... *[Interestingly, not all agree that ...]*

It is important to note ... *[It is important to note that some disagree with ...]*

On the other hand...

Conversely ...

Example of a However Paragraph

◇◇◇◇◇◇◇

Disney World is the best theme park in the world. Although most people refer to "Disney World" as one destination, Disney World is actually comprised of a group of theme parks in Orlando, FL: Magic Kingdom, Epcot, Hollywood Studios, Animal Kingdom, and the water parks: Typhoon Lagoon and Blizzard Beach. In 2016 alone, 20.4 million people visited the Magic Kingdom, the most well-known Disney theme park in Orlando, FL. Disney parks are the best family vacation spots because they offer something for everyone to do. Given the thrill rides and roller coasters, baby rides, interactive family rides, vibrant shows that feature beloved cartoon icons, and not to mention, being able to take pictures with your favorite characters, it is nearly impossible not to have a good time at "The place where dreams come true."

However, deeming Disney World parks as the best theme parks is quite controversial. In fact, some prefer the Universal theme park franchise, which consists of Universal Studios and Islands of Adventure, both located in Orlando, FL. In 2016 alone, almost 10 million people visited Universal Studios Florida. Universal Studios boasts of popular family attractions such as Men In Black: Alien Attack, Transformers: The Ride, and The Wizarding World of Harry Potter. The sister park, Islands of Adventure, also has numerous crowd-pleasing rides, such as The Incredible Hulk. Universal enthusiasts would argue that attending a Universal park is more fun than attending a Disney park.

Chapter 4

The Introduction

You know how everyone wants to make a good first impression? Be it a job interview, a love interest, or moving to a new neighborhood, we want to make sure that our fir st interaction with someone doesn't leave a bad taste in their mouth. Well, the same" concept applies to writing an introduction to a research paper. Th e introduction is the fi rst interaction your professors will have with your work, so give 'em something good. Write something that will pique their interest, something that will lure them in to want to read more.

Beginning in the fi rst grade, I was privileged to attend a highly-ranked, public elementary school in a middle-class neighborhood. My fourth grade Language Arts teacher took her job and her students seriously, so much so that that in preparation for the state writing exam, she trained us as if she were running a boot camp for the Writing Olympics. (And her boot camp was effi cient and effect ive, as her class had the highest number of perfect and near-perfect scores on the state exam.) We wrote an essay every Friday, and as a motivation to pull the best writing out of us, she informed us that when she sat down to grade our papers on Saturday mornings, she would often treat herself to a Krispy Kreme doughnut. She would put the pressure on us, "Your essay should be so good that if your paper is the one that I happen to pick up just as I'm about to go get my donut, that I'd rather finishr eading your narrative over reaching for my doughnut."

In turn, I pass that pressure on to you. Every time you write, your introduction should be so good, so engaging, so intriguing that the reader would choose to read your work over reaching for their favorite, indulgent dessert..

Formula for the Introduction

1) Grasp the reader's attention as soon as she starts reading your paper. Choose one of the following methods, or mix-and-match:

- **Open with dialogue.** Take advantage of people's inclination to eavesdrop by beginning your essay with a conversation. The dialogue could be taking place between real or imagined characters, friends, or foes. It doesn't matter. Conversation is naturally intriguing to the reader.

- **Tell a story.** Provide a personal anecdote about something that happened to you. You could even try telling the story from a bystander, third-person perspective. Who doesn't like to hear a good story?

- **Begin with a quote.** Open your paper with an old adage, quote, or universal truth. It could be well known, obscure, or maybe even something an older relative always says.

> **IMPORTANT**
>
> Whichever method you choose, remember to end the dialogue/story/quote by linking it to the topic of the research paper.

2) Next, clue the reader in on what's to come.

Don't let the reader wander through the weeds and wilderness of your paper alone. Instead, provide a birds-eye view that acts as a roadmap, showing the reader what to expect in your paper. Example:

> *The following analysis will ... [summarize the various viewpoints on X, offer a critique of Y, and conclude with recommendations for future research...]*

Chapter 5

The Conclusion

This chapter provides strategies for the conclusion of your research paper. You can choose one strategy to write your conclusion, or you can combine multiple strategies. The choice is yours. It all depends on the type (and purpose) of the paper you are writing and how long you want your conclusion to be.

1) Summarize your findings.

Remind the reader of the major points in your paper. Be careful! Don't bore the reader by painstakingly repeating, verbatim, everything you just stated. You can avoid boredom by restating the major points clearly, but in a different way. Also, make sure your recap is quick and simple, as you don't want to prolong the conclusion by re-telling, bit by bit, your entire paper.

Depending on the length of your paper, the summary can be as short as one to two sentences, up to one paragraph, or even multiple paragraphs.

2) Conclude with a new revelation.

Be sure to make the teacher/professor aware of any new insight, revelation, or perspective you've gained while completing the research or writing the paper. Here are some suggestions for ending your research paper with a new revelation:

- What major point or new information did you learn while writing?

- Did you develop a new opinion while writing?
- Has your understanding of the topic been broadened? If so, how? What could be an extension of this research?
- Has this research paper made you want to do dig deeper and do even more research? If so, how? And what more do you want to learn?

Chapter 6

Citations

Citations are the academic, formal way to say, "Hey. This is not my idea. I actually got it from ____________." Some citations are "in-text," meaning you insert them into your paper immediately after you state the fact or quote. There are also citations that are placed outside the text, or body, of a research paper. This writing guide will refer to these as "out-of-text citations." Typically, there are two types of out-of-text citations: 1) a reference page that lists all the sources mentioned or cited to, and 2) footnotes (writers use footnotes to include additional information or commentary about something stated in the text).

The format of your research paper depends on your program of study or professor's preference. For the purposes of undergraduate studies, the two, most common formatting styles are:

1. MLA, which stands for "Modern Language Association," and
2. APA, which stands for "American Psychological Association."

Each formatting style has its own rules for how you should write both in-text and out-of-text citations. They also specify how you should format your paper's first page, margins, etc. Your professor should instruct you as to which formatting style she prefers. Typically, such instructions will be included with the assignment, in the syllabus, or during class when the professor is providing instructions about the research assignment. If, however, the professor does not provide such instruction, make sure to ask, "Should we follow MLA or APA?"

In the following pages, I will include examples of both MLA and APA formatting guidelines for in-text and out-of-text citations. However, this writing guide only includes examples of the most common sources (i.e., books, journal articles, etc.). For sources not listed in this guide, you will want to refer directly to the MLA Handbook or the APA Manual. Both are typically available in the library. You can also fi nd formatting rules via online reference websites. (See below, under "Helpful Websites" for examples of helpful websites.)

Other Formatting Styles

This writing guide focuses primarily on MLA and APA formatting. However, there are other formatting guidelines, depending on the field of study and/or profession.

The Bluebook – used for the legal profession and legal academia. (This writing guide briefly covers the Bluebook in Chapter 7.)

Chicago Manual Style – mainly intended for published works (i.e., those published in an academic journal).

IEEE – Institute for Electrical and Electronics Engineers (used in bodies of work concerning engineering, computer science, and technology).

AMA – American Medical Association (used for papers and articles concerning medical research).

Helpful Websites

◇◇◇◇◇◇◇

One motto that I took to heart throughout my time as a student was to "study smarter, not harder." So, before I provide examples of the most common citations, I want to clue you in on some shortcuts that saved me time and frustration.

1) Easybib.com

Easybib was my best friend in high school and college. Whenever I completed my paper and needed to format a Works Cited page, it did it for me. All you have to do is enter basic information about each source, such as type of source (i.e., book, journal article, newspaper, etc.), name of book, article title, date of publication, etc., and *Voila!* Easybib formats the out-of-text citation for you. As of the publication date of this writing guide, Easybib formats MLA out-of-text citations free of charge.

2) The Purdue OWL (owl.purdue.edu)

Whenever Easybib was not of much help, or I had a quick question about how something needed to be formatted, I would google, "how to MLA format ______," or "how to APA format ______." Every time, the Purdue OWL (short for "Online Writing Lab") would pop up, typically with the answer to my question, showing me the correct format. Although this resource will not format the citation for you, as did Easybib, it is really great at clearly outlining how you should format various sources. The Purdue OWL includes information for all the main formatting styles: MLA, APA, the Chicago Manual, IEEE, and AMA.

> If neither Easybib nor the Purdue OWL website helps you, then you will need to review directly the handbook/manual that corresponds to the formatting style you are using.

EXAMPLES

Again, the following are examples of only the most common sources. If your source is not listed in this book, or your question is not answered, please refer directly to the MLA Handbook or APA Publication Manual. (Also, the OWL Purdue website is a very helpful resource.)

MLA

MLA In-text Citations

Include the **author's last name** and **page number**. All of the following formats are acceptable MLA in-text citations:

"Archaeology sheds some light on the foodstuffs consumed by people in biblical times"(Littlejohn 35).

According to Littlejohn, "archaeology sheds some light on the foodstuffs consumed by people in biblical times" (35).

According to Littlejohn, archaeology gives us some idea of what type of food people ate in biblical times (35).

MLA Works Cited

The reference page for an MLA-formatted paper is called a Works Cited page. It lists detailed information for all the sources mentioned. It should be located at the end of your research paper.

General Formatting Guidelines

- Begin the Works Cited on a new page located at the end of your research paper.
- Title the page: Works Cited, centered at the top of the page. Do not bold or italicize the title.
- Double space, but do not skip an additional line between each entry.
- Works cited entries should be listed in alphabetical order.
- All entries must end with a period.
- Each entry should be formatted with a hanging indent. Meaning, after the first line, the subsequent lines should be indented one-half inch from the left margin. This is done for each entry. Example of a a hanging indent:

Jones, Karen. "Fake name of a very, very long journal article." *Phony Academic Journal of Fake Stuff and Science,* vol. 7, no. 1, 2007, pp. 17-29.

MLA Works Cited Authors

- Author names are written as Last Name, First Name. Add the middle name or middle initial when applicable. Examples:

  Williams, Porsha F.

  Jones, Ryan Dennis

- When there are two authors for one work, only the first author appears with the last name, first name format. After the first author is listed, the subsequent author is listed as first name, last name. This applies to all sources (i.e., books, scholarly journals, newspaper articles, etc.). Examples:

(one author): Doe, Jane. *Name of Book.* Publisher, 2019.

(two authors): Doe, Jane, and Angel Everett. *Name of Book.* Publisher, 2019.

If there are three or more authors, list only the first author (Last Name, First Name) followed by the phrase et al. (Latin for "and others") in place of the subsequent authors' names. Example:

(three authors): Doe, Jane, et al. *Name of book.* Publisher, 2019.

Book

Author(s). *Book Title.* City of Publication, Book Publisher, Publication Date.

Include the City of Publication only if:
- the book was published before 1900,
- the publisher has offices in more than one country, or
- the publisher is unknown in North America

Scholarly Journal

Author(s). "Title of Article." *Title of Journal,* vol. 23, no. 1, 2019, pp.17-23.

Volume Number

Issue Number

APA

◇◇◇◇◇◇◇

APA In-text Citations

When mentioning someone else's idea, include a parenthesis with the **author's last name** and the source's **publication date**. Example:

(Everett, 2017)

APA In-text Citations (Short Quotes)

If, however, you are including a direct quote in your paper, you must include the **author's last name**, the source's **publication date**, and the quote's **page number**.

Example 1:

According to Everett (2017), "How you perform under one teaching method does not dictate your intellectual competency" (p.201).

Example 2:

She stated, "How you perform under one teaching method does not dictate your intellectual competency" (Everett, 2017, p.201), but I disagree.

APA In-text Citations (Block Quotes)

If the quote is long (i.e., forty words or more), then it needs to stand-alone, outside of the rest of the paragraph. Also, for block quotes, omit the quotation marks, and start the quote on a new line. Indent the quote ½ inch from the left margin. Keep this indentation for the entirety of the quoted paragraph. Double-space. Example:

In *Harvard and Hardship: A Beginner's Guide to College and Law School,* Everett (2017) suggested:

> If you want to speak up, then speak up. Know that your experiences, insight, and opinions are valuable, just as valuable as that of anyone else in the classroom. However, if you don't want to speak up, then don't, and don't feel obligated to "illuminate" someone. Either way, be at peace with your choice. (p. 202)

APA Reference List

The APA reference list is where you will include detailed information for all of the sources mentioned in the research paper. It should be located at the end of your research paper.

Reference List Format

- Begin the reference list on a new page located at the end of your research paper.
- Title the reference list: **References**, in bold, centered at the top of the reference list.
- Double space.
- List the entries in alphabetical order. (Alphabetize the entries using the last name of the first author of each work.)
- Each work should be formatted with a hanging indent. Meaning, after the first line, the subsequent lines of that work should be indented one-half inch from the left margin. Do this for every work on the reference list. Example of a hanging indent:

Author, J.B. (Year of Publication). *Title of work: This is the very long subtitle of the book.* Publisher.

APA Reference List Formatting Examples

Book (single author)

See the section, "APA Reference List Authors," for examples of how to format works with multiple authors.

Author, A. B. (Year of publication). *Title of work: Capital letter also for subtitle* (E. Editor, Ed.). Publisher.

If the book was edited, include the editor's information: Initial of the First Name, Full Last Name, then "Ed." (Ed. is short for "Editor.")

Scholarly Journal (in print)

Author, A.A., Author, B.B., & Author, C.C. (2015). Article Name. *Journal of Blah Blah Blah,* 55(2), 893-896.

Volume Number

Issue Number

Page numbers wherein the article is located

Scholarly Journal (electronic)

Author, A.A., Author, B. B., & Author, C. C. (2015). Article Name. *Journal of Blah Blah Blah, 55*(2), 893-896. https://doi.org/12.345/6789

When referencing an article from a periodical (i.e, from a scholarly or academic journal), include the doi number of the article, if available. If no doi is provided (and you accessed the article from online), then use the url of the website from where you retrieved the journal article.

55 refers to the volume number of the journal.

2 refers to the issue number. (Include if applicable.)

893-896 are the pages wherein the article is located.

APA Reference List Authors

- List authors by including their last name and initials of their first and middle names. Example:

  Everett, A. R.

- When there are two authors, use "&" to separate the two names. Still list authors by their last name and initials of their first and middle names. Example:

  Jones, A.S., & Becker, C.P. (2016). Awesome Article. *Fake Academic and Scholarly Journal, 34*(2), 1-7. http://dx.doi.org/00.0000/jn000000

- Three to twenty authors:

  List all authors as Last Name, First Name Initial. Middle Name Initial. Example:

  Knowles, B. G., Everett, A. R., Battles, N. K., Jones, T. A., Richardson, T. B., & Davis, J. T. (2018). Article Title. *Journal Name, 54*(1), 9-19. http://dx.doi.org/00.0000/jn000000

- 21 or more authors:

  After the 19th author use an ellipsis (…) (but no "&"), and then add the final author's name. Do not list more than 20 authors. Example:

  Knowles, B. G., Everett, A. R., Battles, N. K., Navarez, T. A., Richardson, T. B., Davis, J. T., Smith, A., Rodgers, C., Patel, P., Jemison, K., Rodriguez, C., Perino, A., Gonzales, F., Wigglesworth, S., Kuhlman, K., Jones, T.B., Pierre, J., Locklear, Y. T., Lewis, R. H., …Nguyen, L. (2018). Article Title. *Journal Name, 54*(1), 9-19. http://dx.doi.org/00.0000/jn000000

PART B

Law School

> Law school writing is distinctively different from any other college or university writing.

Part B provides some guidelines I wish I would have known before entering law school. Note, the following insight provides only a basic lay of the land, so you will not feel as lost as I did my first semester of law school. Ultimately, you will need to refer to your professor or supervisor for her expectations and specific subject-matter questions.

Chapter 7

Legal Citations (The Bluebook)

I remember the first time I read a case in law school. I was reading along when all of a sudden I saw: *See Doe v. Texas,* 60 F.3d 190, 191 (2012). I kept reading the case, only to come across another command, coupled with another string of letters and numbers: *But see Jones v. Ropes*, 892 U.S. 34 (1999).

Must be some legal stuff, I thought. I kept reading, allowing my mind to mindlessly brush over the intermittent strings of letters and numbers to get to the meat of the case.

Then, the dreaded second-thought knocked me back to my high-achiever senses:

> *Wait, this is* ***LAW*** *school. Shouldn't I understand the* ***LEGAL*** *stuff?*
>
> *Why don't I know what that means? Am I supposed to know?*
>
> *Isn't this glancing-game bad?*

What I eventually learned was that those random notes to "see" followed by a seemingly random assembly of numbers were legal citations, informing me of the source from where the information in the preceding sentence had come. It was a reference to where I could go to do more research, or even what case (or other written work) was in opposition to something just stated.

Sources, Authorities, and the Bluebook

◇◇◇◇◇◇◇

Note that legal sources that present legal rules, legal doctrine, or legal reasoning are referred to as legal ***authorities*** in law school and the legal profession. So, whether you are citing to a case opinion, a code of regulations, or even a law review article, you are citing to an authority. Moving forward, we will refer to legal sources as authorities.

Not only will you see citations as you read cases, but also you will need to create your own citations when you write legal analyses for your legal research and writing class. Meaning, when you write a legal memo or legal brief, you will need to include citations formatted according to the rules outlined in the Bluebook.

The Bluebook, simply put, is a book of all the rules for formatting legal citations. It has instructions for how to cite and abbreviate almost any authority: from cases and books to congressional hearings, to abbreviations for the names of courts and states – the Bluebook has a certain way the citations and abbreviations should be formatted.

Although the Bluebook has thousands of rules, here are the most common citation forms that will come in handy in law school.

Case

◇◇◇◇◇◇◇

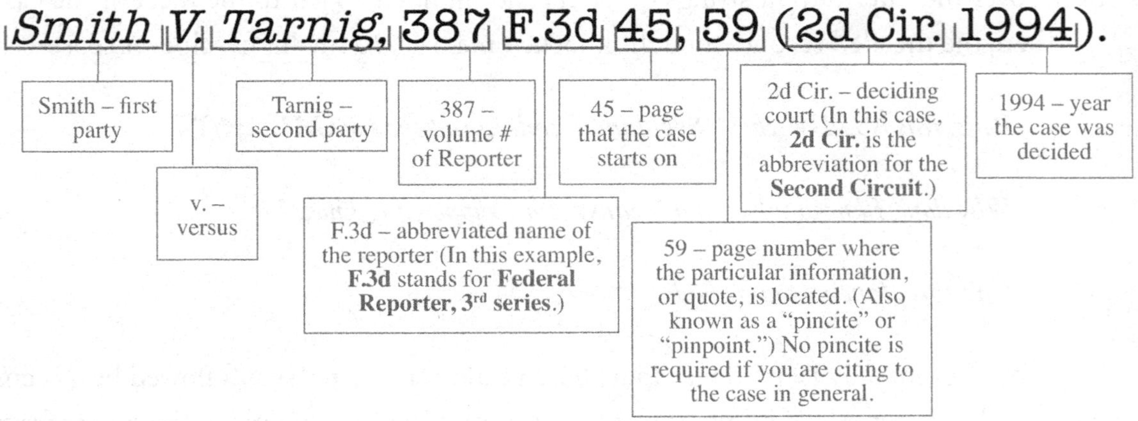

<u>CASE (U.S. SUPREME COURT)</u>

◇◇◇◇◇◇◇◇

If the case is from the U.S. Supreme Court, the citation will be a bit different:

***Pollard* v. *Company*, 32 U.S. 3, 8 (2017).**

- Pollard – first party
- v. – versus
- Company – second party
- 32 – volume # of reporter
- 3 – page that the case starts on
- 2017 – year the case was decided (no court is listed because it is clear, from the reporter name, that this is a decision from the U.S. Supreme Court)
- U.S. – name of reporter (Reporter – imagine it to be a book where the case is archived. In this example, **U.S.** is the abbreviation for **United States Reports**, which is the official Supreme Court reporter.)
- 8 – page number where the particular information, or quote, is located (Also known as a **pincite**, or **pinpoint**. No pincite is required if you are citing the case in general.)

<u>CASE (WITH PARENTHETICAL EXPLANATION)</u>

◇◇◇◇◇◇◇◇

Occasionally, the citation will include a parenthetical. The parenthetical usually provides a summary of the case, or some other pertinent information regarding the case.

- F.3d – abbreviated name of reporter (In this example, **F.3d** stands for **Federal Reporter, 3rd series**.)
- 2d Cir. – deciding court (In this case, **2d Cir.** is the abbreviation for the **Second Circuit**.)
- United States – first party
- v. – versus
- Solomon – second party
- 432 – volume number of reporter
- 23 – first page of case
- 48-52 – range of pages that were referenced
- 2011 – year of decision

***United States* v. *Solomon*, 432 F.3d 23, 48-52 (2d Cir. 2011) (held that a certain law means blah, blah, blah).**

- Parenthetical phrase describing the decision of the Second Circuit

CASE (SHORT FORM)

◇◇◇◇◇◇◇

Use the short form to cite to a case only after it has been cited in full elsewhere in the document.

So, for instance, the short form for *United States v. Solomon* (the last citation example located on the previous page) would be:

***Solomon*, 432 F.3d at 49.**

Solomon – shortened case name (In this example, the government is also a party to this case. However, do NOT use the governmental party in the shortform. Instead, use the name of the other party to the suit.)

volume number and reporter abbreviation

include the specific page referred to using the construction **at #.**

BOOK

◇◇◇◇◇◇◇

page cited

Ariana B. Doolittle, *Title of book* 65 (John B. Doe et al. eds., 7th ed. 2017).

Editor's name; In this example, there is more than one editor. Hence, **et al. eds.** is the abbreviation for **editors**. If there is only one editor, omit **et al. eds.** If the editor name is unavailable, no worries. Omit this section of the citation. Include only the edition number and year of publication in the parenthesis.

Edition cited If only one edition of the book exists, omit this portion of the citation.

Year of publication

PERIODICAL (I.E., LAW REVIEW ARTICLES, SCHOLARLY JOURNALS, ETC.)

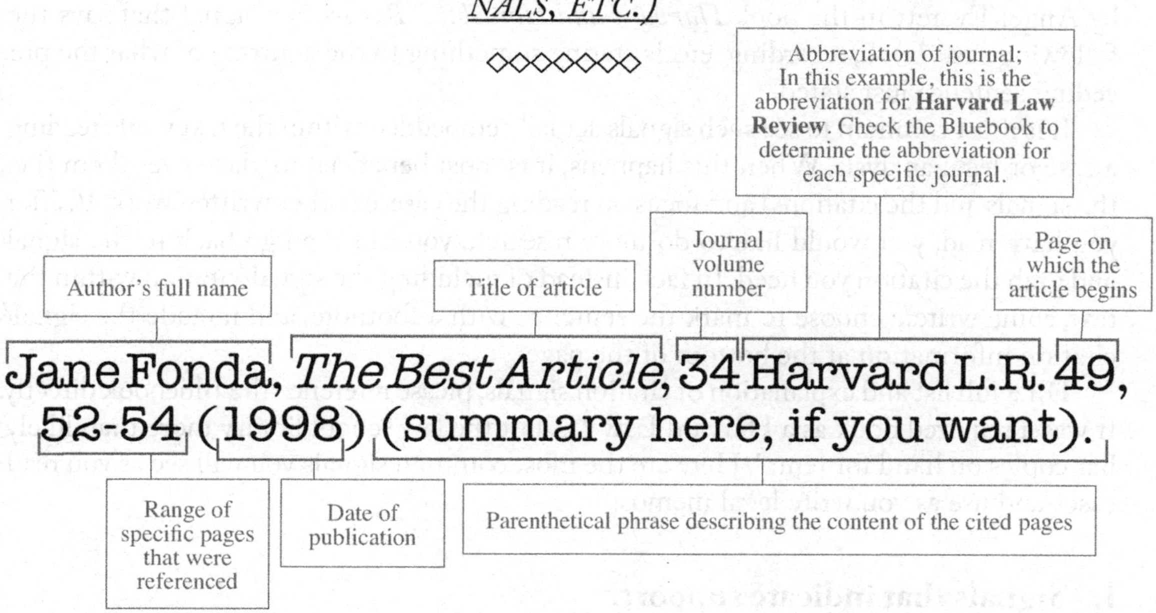

SIGNALS

Aside from the citations, there are also "signals." Signals are typically in front of a citation, and they provide instruction about the citation. Specifically, they answer one (and sometimes multiple) of the following questions: Why is the citation useful? Why is the writer listing the citation? What is the purpose of the citation?

EXAMPLE

According to the Mythical Tradition of Law School, law school is extremely difficult, and only a pre-selected, elite group of people can be successful at it. *But see* Angel Everett, *Harvard and Hardship: A Beginner's Guide to College and Law School* (2017).

In the example above, "*But see*" is saying, "But look at this contrasting opinion, offered by Angel Everett in the book *Harvard and Hardship*." *But see* is a signal that says the following case, book, recording, etc. is stating something to the contrary of what the preceding sentence just stated.

It is most common to see such signals actually embedded within the text while reading a case or legal analysis. When this happens, it is most beneficial to glaze over them (i.e., the signals and the citations) and focus on reading the case, or other written work. If, after you have read, you would like to do more research, you can then go back to the signal and grab the citation you need. In fact, instead of including the signal/citation within the text, some writers choose to mark the sentence with a footnote, and include the signal/citation information at the bottom of the page.

For a full list and explanation of citation signals, please reference the Bluebook directly. It was a required book as a Harvard Law 1L, but the law school library more than likely has copies on hand for rental. Here are the most common signals you will see as you read cases and use as you write legal memos.

I. Signals that indicate support.

No signal

Sometimes while reading, you will come across a citation with no signal. Meaning, there will be a sentence, immediately followed by a citation.

Example

In *Florida v. The World*, it was held that Florida is the best state to live and vacation in. *Florida v. The World*, 49 U.S. 45, 34 (2017).

Use [no signal] when you referred to an authority in the preceding sentence, and the citation simply identifies the authority. So, for instance, in the above example, the sentence already references the case ***Florida v. The World***. Hence, no signal is needed because the citation is merely providing specific citation information about the authority. Also use [no signal] when the preceding sentence provides a direct quotation from the authority, or when restating numerical data from the authority.

See

◇◇◇◇◇◇◇

See is used when the cited authority does not, word for word, state the assertion in the preceding sentence, but if the reader were to check the cited authority, it would be clear that it supports the assertion.

See is slightly different from [no signal]. Whereas [no signal] indicates that the cited authority states the proposition exactly, *see* indicates that the cited authority may not ***directly*** state the proposition, but that the cited authority still clearly supports the proposition. Example:

U.S. history is rooted in the notion of equality. For instance, Black men, White men, Native American men, Latino men, and Asian men should be treated equally. *See* The Declaration of Independence para. 2 (U.S. 1776).

The Declaration of Independence does not exactly make mention of all the different races of men listed in the above assertion. Hence, [*no signal*] cannot be used; a signal is necessary. The Declaration of Independence states that "all men are created equal." The assertion that Black men, White men, Native American men, Latino men, and Asian men are equal is, therefore, a logical statement that naturally follows from the Declaration of Independence's statement that "all men are created equal." *See* indicates that the Declaration of Independence supports the assertion about the different races.

II. Signals that indicate contradiction or opposition.

Contra

◇◇◇◇◇◇◇

Contra indicates that the cited authority **states the direct opposite** of what was just asserted in the text.

All men were not created equally. *Contra* The Declaration of Independence para. 2 (U.S. 1776).

The U.S. Declaration of Independence (which states that "all men are created equal") **states the exact opposite** of the assertion that "all men were not created equally." Therefore, the *contra* signal is appropriate here.

But See

◇◇◇◇◇◇◇

But see indicates that the cited authority **supports a conclusion that is contrary** to what was just asserted in the text. Difference between *contra* and *but see*: Use *contra* when the authority includes a statement that is the exact opposite of what was asserted in the text. Use *but see* when the authority is generally contrary to what was asserted in the text, but there is no clear statement asserting the exact opposite; An additional inferential step is necessary to infer that the authority is in disagreement with the in-text assertion.

Tall men are superior to short men. *But see* The Declaration of Independence para. 2 (U.S. 1776).

But see is appropriate here because the cited authority, the Declaration of Independence, does not contain a clear statement asserting the opposite of what was asserted in the text. Meaning, the Declaration of Independence does not explicitly state, "It is not true that tall men are superior to short men." However, the Declaration of Independence does support a conclusion (all men are equal) that is contrary to the statement that "tall men are superior to short men."

Id.

◇◇◇◇◇◇◇

This signal means, "The citation for what I just stated is the same citation that I just used, and according to the Bluebook, I don't have to rewrite the citation again. I can just write *Id.*" Use *Id.* to avoid retyping the citation every time you make an assertion from the same authority that you ***last*** cited to. **Only use *Id.* if the authority for the current statement is the same authority that was just *last cited.*** Otherwise, type out the full citation.

EXAMPLE

The sky is blue. *See* Astrid Sanchez, *Obvious Article*, Fake Encyclopedia of the Obvious 73, 75 (2018). Although it is obvious that the sky is blue, it is interesting to note that sometimes, it is dark grey, especially when a storm is impending. Moreover, it turns black at night. Also, grass is usually green. *Id.* at 78. Of course, however, if the grass is not watered properly, it may turn brown.

In the above example, "*Id.* at 78," notifies the reader that the proposition that "grass is usually green" came from the Obvious Article, and that it came specifically from p. 78 of the Obvious Article. Notice that you can still use *Id.*, as long as you are citing to the same authority again, even if the page number changes.

Again, Only use *Id.* if the authority for the current statement is the same as the immediately preceding cited authority. Otherwise, type out the full citation.

EXAMPLE

The sky is blue. *See* Astrid Sanchez, *Obvious Article*, Fake Encyclopedia of the Obvious 73, 75 (2018). Although it is obvious that the sky is blue, it is interesting to note that sometimes, it is dark grey, especially when a storm is impending. Moreover, it turns black at night. There have been no recorded sightings of the sky being hot pink. Joel Malango, *Cool Weather Sightings*, 24 Weather Journal 89, 3 (2007). Also, grass is usually green. *See* Astrid Sanchez, *Obvious Article*, Fake Encyclopedia of the Obvious 73, 75 (2018). Of course, however, if the grass is not watered properly, it may turn brown.

There are three citations in the above passage:

1st – to the *Obvious Article*

2nd – to *Cool Weather Sightings*

3rd – to the *Obvious Article*

The citation to *Cool Weather Sightings* interrupted the continuity of citing to the *Obvious Article*. Hence, *Id.* could not be used when the *Obvious Article* was cited to again.

CHAPTER 8

LAW SCHOOL EXAMS

A WORD ABOUT OUTLINES

Outlines are the staple of the law school experience. As outlined in *Harvard and Hardship: A Beginner's Guide to College and Law School*, I categorize outlines into two types:

- Daily Class Outline – includes summaries of all the cases for the class, as well as other major insights such as history and context.

- Exam Outline – includes only the rules from the class. Rules may be from cases, statutes, and/or regulations.

Daily class outlines are typically much longer than exam outlines. I felt most confident about the exams that I prepared for using an exam outline. During the exam, you will not have time to flip through the daily class outline to find the rule statement you need. For most law school exams, certain parts of the daily class outline (namely, the judges' legal reasoning and the historical context) are superfluous when it comes time to take the test. On the other hand, the exam outline, which looks like a list of rules categorized thematically, will act as a quick and convenient go-to that you will reference while writing your exam. After all, for most law school exams, one thing reigns supreme: the rule statement.

What does the law say? For this reason, if it is an open-note exam, I suggest taking the exam with an exam outline.

Outlines are a bit controversial in law school. Some in legal academia say students should create their own outlines. And I agree – the ability to synthesize the information into a well-organized, thematic-based summary of the class shows an advanced level of comprehension. However, I remember attempting to make my own outlines as a first semester 1L and totally not having a clue what I was doing. I felt like I was shooting in the dark. *But hey*, I thought, *At least I'm creating my own outlines. That's what matters most, right?*

Wrong.

In retrospect, as a student with no prior exposure to legal analysis, law school, or legal writing, I would have been better off if, at least for that first semester, I would have stuck with a pre-made exam outline and taken multiple practice tests using that outline. There is a particular format and rationale behind creating law school outlines. Because I was ignorant of the prescribed format and rationale, my first outlines did not present the information in an effective, thematic fashion; they included things that were unnecessary, and they left out major points. Although I was willing and diligent, I had no idea what I was doing. How can we expect unexposed students, who may be the first in their families or, moreover, *communities*, to enter this realm of education, to telepathically know how to create an outline? Hence, I advise first-semester 1Ls (or even second semester 1Ls, if you feel like you still need those training wheels), to study using pre-made outlines. Specifically, use the daily class outline throughout the semester to help guide and bring focus to your reading. Then, as the exam period approaches, use the exam outline to take multiple practice tests for each course.

Most of our exams at Harvard Law were open-note, so I was usually able to take the exam outline into the test with me. However, even if your school/professor has a closed-note, closed-book exam policy, studying with an exam outline is still helpful because it trains your mind to think in terms of the rules. Also, you can create two-column notes, and/or flashcards based on the rules, cases, regulations, etc. outlined in the exam outline.

There are two main types of written* law school exams: The Issue Spotter, and The Policy Question.

Of course, some professors will include multiple choice, fill-in-the blank, and other methods to test the course material. However, this chapter provides information for the two traditional, most common types of **written law school exams.*

The Issue Spotter

◇◇◇◇◇◇◇◇

The Issue Spotter is the traditional, most common type of law school exam. Here is how it works: The professor gives you a "fact pattern." A fact pattern is a story about the escapades, tragedies, and sometimes good fortunes of the fictional character(s). Although the fact pattern tells a story, the story is actually a bunch of legal issues, and your job is to read the fact pattern with laser beam eyes to spot all the relevant legal issues (that is, those issues that are relevant to the subject matter of the class). Once you spot the issues, your next task is to analyze each issue and conclude how the court is likely to rule.

How to approach Issue-Spotter exams

◇◇◇◇◇◇◇◇

Begin by reading the fact pattern. Glance it over, just to get a feel for the storyline and the general area of law the professor is testing. Also, be sure to review the "call of the question." The call of the question is the prompt – what is the professor asking you to do?

Then, go back and read the fact pattern. This time as you read, circle (or list) issues that "jump out" at you. Don't worry about the analysis or how the issues should be resolved; just make note of what stands out to you.

As I have stated before, legal writing is different from undergraduate, or even other graduate-level writing. Flowery words, eloquent diction, and/or an engaging introduction will probably not get you bonus points. On the contrary, law school writing is very formulaic. The formula I learned at Harvard Law is best memorized as an acrostic poem, "IRAC" (pronounced, "eye – rack)"

I – Issue. Name the issue.

This can be stated in one sentence. (*The issue is…*) Alternatively, simply listing the issue as the heading, or subtitle, of the paragraph is also sufficient.

R – Rule. State the rule.

What does the law say? Here is where you will reference your exam outline (for open-note exams). For closed exams, you will have to reference your memory.

A – Application, or Analysis. Apply the rule to the facts.

What does the rule statement (from above) have to say about these specific facts?

C – Conclusion. Based on your analysis, state how a court would rule.

What would be the outcome?

IRAC EXAMPLE

FACT PATTERN EXCERPT

◇◇◇◇◇◇◇◇

One day, Ashley was strolling in the marketplace when she came across a stand of delicious red apples. Spotting an admirable five-year-old little boy ("Jamaal") nearby, she takes one of the apples from the stand and hands it to Jamaal.

"Aw, thanks, Ashley! You're the best!" Jamaal gleefully exclaims as he voraciously devours the apple.

After helping another customer, the owner of the fruit stand jumps in front of Ashley and screams, "You thief! You didn't pay for that!"

Ashley responds, "I sure didn't! And there's nothing you can do about it!"

Suddenly Cody barges in and explains, "Please forgive my sister. She has been diagnosed with a mental illness."

"Yeah, right!" screeches the owner of the fruit stand. "I'm calling the cops! Both her and the little boy are guilty of stealing!"

Identify the criminal charges likely to be brought and possible defenses.

Example Plan

◇◇◇◇◇◇◇◇

Remember: Issue. Rule. Application. Conclusion.

1) ASHLEY

Elements of a Crime
Actus Reus
I – Actus Reus. Was there a criminal act?
R – An act is a physical act (or unlawful omission). For there to be criminal liability, the defendant must have either performed a voluntary physical act or failed to act under circumstances that imposed a legal duty to act.
A – Ashley acted when she took the apple from the fruit stand.
C – The act requirement has been met.

Mens Rea
I – Mens rea. Did Ashley have a guilty mind?
R – Mens rea is a guilty mind. It refers to the state of mind or intent of the defendant at the time of her act. One acts with purpose when they act with intent that their act causes a certain result. One acts with knowledge when they are aware that their action will lead to a certain result. One acts recklessly when they are aware that there is a substantial risk of their action leading to a certain result. One acts negligently if they should have been aware of the substantial and unjustifiable risk created by their action.
A – Ashley took the apple from the stand with the intent not to pay for it. Her intention not to pay for the apple was evidenced when she responds to the fruit stand owner's accusation of not paying for the apple with, "I sure didn't!"
C – Ashley acted with purpose.

Larceny
I – Larceny
R – Common law larceny requires a wrongful taking, or carrying away, of the property of another by trespass with intent to permanently deprive.
A – Ashley carried away the apple. The apple did not rightfully belong to Ashley, but it was the property of the fruit stand's owner. Since Ashley gave the apple to someone

else to eat, it can be reasonably assumed she intended to permanently deprive the owner of the fruit stand from his apple.
C – Ashley has committed larceny.

Defenses
I – Insanity
R – M'Naghten rule: At the time of her conduct, Defendant lacked the ability to know the wrongfulness of her actions or understand the nature and quality of her actions.

Irresistible Impulse rule: Defendant lacked the capacity for self-control and free choice.

Durham rule: Defendant's conduct was a product of mental illness or mental disease.

Model Penal Code: the defendant lacked substantial capacity either to appreciate the criminality of their conduct or to conform their conduct to the requirements of the law.

A – M'Naghten rule: When Ashley took the apple, she lacked the ability to know that taking the apple from the stand and giving it to Nick was wrong. She did not understand that it was wrong to take something that did not belong to her.

Irresistible Impulse rule: Ashley could not stop herself from taking the apple. She lacked self-control. It was not her own choice to take the apple.

Durham rule: Ashley's brother, Cody, mentioned that Ashley "suffers from a diagnosed mental illness."

Model Penal Code: Ashley was unable to conform her conduct (i.e., taking the apple) to the law (i.e., that one must pay for the apple in order to take it).

C – Whether or not Ashely has a successful insanity defense depends on the jurisdiction where the charges are brought and which test for insanity that jurisdiction uses.

> *Note: write a conclusion for each insanity defense. Also, conclude which insanity defense would hold up the best.*

2) JAMAAL

Accomplice Liability (Larceny)
I – Is Jamaal criminally liable for larceny on a theory of accomplice liability?
R – An accomplice is one who aids, advises, or encourages the principal in the commission of the crime charged.
A – Jamaal accepted and ate the apple that Ashley, the principal, gave him. He did not "aid" her in the alleged crime because by the time he accepted the apple, the criminal

offense had already been committed. Ashley had already taken the apple from the fruit stand. Also, the facts do not indicate that he advised or encouraged Ashley to take the apple.
C – Jamaal was not an accomplice to Ashley's larceny.

Infancy Defense
I – Is infancy a viable defense for Jamaal?
R – In most jurisdictions, there is no criminal liability for defendants under the age of seven.
A – Jamaal is five years old.
C – Infancy is a viable defense for Jamaal.

Example Written Essay Response

For an issue spotter exam, your exam will essentially be a series of "IRACs."

1) ASHLEY

Elements of a crime

In analyzing whether Ashley is liable for any particular crime, it is necessary to first determine if the elements of a crime have been met. Both the criminal act element and the guilty mind element must be concurrently met for the individual to be charged with the crime.

Actus Reus

An act is a physical act (or unlawful omission) by the defendant. For there to be criminal liability, the defendant must have either performed a voluntary physical act or failed to act under circumstances that imposed a legal duty to act. Ashley acted when she took the apple from the fruit stand. Therefore, the act requirement has been met.

Mens Rea

Mens rea refers to the state of mind or intent of the defendant at the time of her act. One acts with purpose when they act with intent that their act causes a certain result. One acts with knowledge when they are aware that their action will lead to a certain result. One acts recklessly when they are aware that there is a substantial risk of their action leading to a certain result. One acts negligently if they should have been aware of the substantial and unjustifiable created by their action. Ashley took the apple from the stand with the intent not to pay for it. Her intention not to pay for the apple was evidenced when she responds to the fruit stand owner's accusation of not paying for the apple with, "I sure didn't!" Therefore, Ashley acted with purpose.

Larceny

Common law larceny requires a wrongful taking or carrying away of the property of another by trespass with intent to permanently deprive. Ashley carried away the apple. The apple did not rightfully belong to her, but it was the property of the owner of the fruit stand. Since Ashley gave the apple to someone else to eat, it can be reasonably assumed she intended to permanently deprive the owner of the fruit stand from his apple. Therefore, Ashley has committed larceny.

Insanity Defense

If the cases progresses, Ashley will likely try to plead insanity. The rule for insanity differs according to the jurisdiction wherein the charges are brought.

The M'Naghten rule states that at the time of her conduct, Defendant lacked the ability to know the wrongfulness of her actions or understand the nature and quality of her actions.) If charges are brought in a M'Naghten jurisdiction, Ashley could argue that when she took the apple, she lacked the ability to know that taking the apple from the stand and giving it to Nick was wrong. Provided that she is able to provide credible evidence of an inability to appreciate the wrongfulness of her action, insanity could be a viable defense in a M'Naghten jurisdiction.

The Irresistible Impulse rule states that the Defendant lacked the capacity for self-control and free choice. If charges are brought in an "irresistible impulse" jurisdiction, Ashley would have to show that she lacked self-control, and it was not her own choice to take the apple. Based on the facts provided, however, this does not seem like a viable defense.

The Durham rule states that the Defendant's conduct was a product of mental illness. If charges are brought in a Durham jurisdiction, Ashley must show that taking the apple and giving it to Nick was the product of a mental illness. Given that Cody, Ashley's brother, mentioned that Ashley "suffers from a diagnosed mental illness," insanity would be a viable defense in a jurisdiction that uses the Durham rule.

The Model Penal Code requires that the defendant lacked substantial capacity either to appreciate the criminality of their conduct or to conform their conduct to the requirements of the law. Cody mentioned that Ashley has a diagnosed mental illness, however, in order to have a viable insanity defense in an MPC jurisdiction, Ashley would have to show that her mental illness made her lack substantial capacity to appreciate the criminality of taking the apple without paying for it, OR Ashley would have to show that she lacked substantial capacity to conform her conduct (i.e., taking an apple from a marketplace) to the law (i.e., that one must pay for an apple that they take from a marketplace). Based on the facts provided, Ashley probably has a viable insanity defense under the MPC definition of insanity.

2) JAMAAL

Accomplice Liability for Larceny

An accomplice is one who aids, advises, or encourages the principal in the commission of the crime charged. Jamaal accepted (and ate) the apple that Ashley, the principal, gave him. He did not "aid" her in the alleged crime because by the time he had accepted the apple, the criminal offense had already been committed – Ashley had already taken the apple from the fruit stand. Also, the facts do not indicate that Jamaal advised or encouraged Ashley to take the apple. Therefore, Jamaal was not an accomplice to Ashley's larceny.

Infancy Defense

For most jurisdictions, there is no criminal liability for individuals under the age of seven. Jamaal was five years old when he accepted the apple from Ashley. He is, therefore, under the age of majority. In the event that the State attempts to hold Jamaal criminally liable for larceny, infancy is a viable defense for him.

The Issue Spotter: Tips and Tricks

◇◇◇◇◇◇◇

- **Take practice exams.** Make sure to get your hands on past prior exams and model answers from that particular class and professor a few weeks prior to the exam. 1) Start studying by first reviewing the exam and the model answer. 2) Then, study by taking a practice exam and reviewing the model answer ***after*** you have tried to answer yourself. 3) After writing out 1-2 exams, you can take the remaining practice exams by simply outlining how you would answer. Meaning, list the issues, and write one-sentence, bullet-points answers for the IRACs. You don't want to tire yourself out by writing out multiple, full-length exams before the actual exam.

- **Pay attention to the "call" of the question**. Do not overthink it. Do not overanalyze. Do exactly what it tells you to do. Sometimes the call will be as straightforward as "identify and analyze the legal issues and likely outcomes." In that case, the call is simply asking you to IRAC all the issues in the fact pattern.

Other times, however, the call will ask you to form an overall conclusion of the overall fact pattern. If this is the case, the overall conclusion may not be evident until after you IRAC all the issues. So, in this case, 1) First, IRAC each issue. 2) Once you have "worked out" all the IRACs, take a step back and review them. What is the overall outcome? Yes, this means you will actually go through and complete the bulk of your response before reaching the final conclusion, but no worries. Don't sweat it. Just write your conclusion at the end of your exam, after you have taken time to consider all your IRACs.

Here are some examples of issue spotter "calls," along with an interpretation of what the professor is asking you to do:

- *Identify and analyze the legal issues and likely outcomes.* – Spot each issue. IRAC each issue.
- *Analyze the legal issues and present a conclusion to how the court should rule.* – Spot each issue. IRAC each issue. Then, consider each IRAC in context of the big picture, and present an overall conclusion at the end.
- *Identify the criminal charges the District Attorney will likely bring against each individual, as well as possible defenses. (criminal law exam)* – Spot each issue. IRAC each criminal offense. For each identified criminal offense, IRAC each possible criminal defense.
- *What are the various liabilities of the parties involved? Any defenses? (torts or contracts exam)* – Spot each issue. IRAC each issue. For each identified issue, IRAC each possible defense.

- **Don't worry about getting the "right" conclusion**. I know this sounds counter-intuitive, but this is simply how Issue Spotter exams go. Spotting issues and IRAC'ing them should give you sufficient points, even if you don't come out with the "right" answer in your conclusion. Professors care more about your analysis and thoughtful consideration of how the law interacts with the provided facts, rather than whether you came out with the "right" conclusion. That goes both for the conclusion portion of the IRAC, as well as the overall conclusion of your exam.

- **Give each character their own IRAC.** When you see multiple characters in the fact pattern, don't huff and puff and have a panic attack. This is actually a good thing; it is an opportunity for you to score more points. The call of the question may ask you to, for instance, "identify criminal offenses and possible defenses for each individual." In this example, each individual should have their own set of IRACs: IRACs for their crimes and IRACs for possible defenses. Example:

1) Julie

Criminal Offenses
IRAC crime #1
IRAC crime #2
IRAC crime #3

Possible Defenses
IRAC defense #1
IRAC defense #2

2) Mateo

Criminal Offenses
IRAC crime #1
IRAC crime #2
IRAC crime #3

Possible Defenses
IRAC defense #1
IRAC defense #2

3) Prisha

Criminal Offenses
IRAC crime #1
IRAC crime #2
IRAC crime #3

<u>Possible Defenses</u>
IRAC defense #1
IRAC defense #2

- **Go for the low-hanging fruit first.** When you take an issue-spotter exam, don't get caught up trying to find all the tricks, hidden issues, and extra-analyses. Professors purposely include tons of issues for you to spot, so that you have ample opportunity to gain points. So, if an issue jumps out at you, mark it as something you will address, and keep reading for the next issue. Don't get stuck re-reading one paragraph of the fact pattern trying to read between the lines. Doing so will cost you precious time and points.

  Instead, as you take more and more practice tests, and compare the exemplar response to your response, you will begin to see patterns: First, you'll see the main issues (i.e., the low-hanging fruit) that are "giveaways," but as you take more and more practice exams you will also begin to see the "hidden" issues and opportunities to delve deeper into the analysis. However, I caution you – <u>**First**</u> develop a comfort with identifying the basic issues and completing basic IRACs. I cannot say it enough: you will get better at spotting issues (and opportunities for deeper analysis) over time. I have included guidelines on how to do those deeper analyses in the latter portion of this section, but give yourself time. I remember I failed my 1L civil procedure exam because I was too busy trying to find all the tricks, hidden issues, and showcase some (nonexistent at the time) legal analysis. DO NOT DO THAT. It's not worth it. I'm sure I would have at least passed that exam if I had just focused on the main issues, completed the basic IRAC for each issue, and kept it moving.

- **Point to what different jurisdictions would do.** (This is one of those opportunities to show a more complex analysis in your IRAC.) Many times, different states have slightly different rules and ways to deal with a criminal offense or civil liability. As you IRAC each issue, make note in the "rule" section if different jurisdictions have a different rule. If so, make sure to mention the different rule in your analysis. Also, in the "Application/Analysis" section of the IRAC, make mention of how the "other" jurisdiction's law would handle the facts. Doing so takes your legal analysis up a notch and reigns in more points!

  It will be evident whether or not this type of analysis is relevant to the course, because, during the lectures/in your outlines, the professor will have mentioned the different jurisdictions' versions of the law. If the professor never makes such mention, then this analysis is not meant for that class exam. Personally, this type of jurisdictional-based analysis was relevant to my torts and criminal law classes.

- **Point to the difference (if any) between the common law rule and a rule based on a statute, regulation, or code**. (This is another opportunity to show a more complex analysis in your IRAC.) There are different ways that laws are formed. Some laws are based on "common law" (i.e., when the rule is formed by case law). Other laws are based on statute, regulation, or a code.

  Many times during class, my criminal law professor would point out if the common law differed from the "Model Penal Code." If applicable to your fact pattern, use the "rule" section of the IRAC to make a quick mention of the difference between the two authorities (sources) of law. Then, use the "application/analysis" section to apply both the common law rule and the statute-based, or code-based rule to the facts. Doing so (when applicable) shows a higher level of analysis and should score you extra points.

  Again, please note that it will be evident whether or not this type of analysis is relevant to the course, because, during the lectures (and/or in your outlines), the professor will have mentioned differences in the common law rule vs. another rule source. If the professor never makes such mention, then this analysis is not meant for that course exam. Personally, this type of "common law rule vs. statute/regulatory rule" analysis was relevant to my Criminal Law class (Common Law vs. the Model Penal Code) and Contracts class (Common Law vs. The Universal Commercial Code).

THE POLICY QUESTION

◇◇◇◇◇◇◇

Another type of written law school exam is the Policy Question. Whereas the purpose of the Issue Spotter is for you to show that you know what the law ***is***, the Policy Question allows you to offer insight into what the law ***should be***. The professor is giving you the opportunity to be the lawmaker, congresswoman, or senator for the day. Hence, whereas with the Issue Spotter, there was no place or need for your opinion or outside knowledge, your opinion and outside knowledge are necessary with the Policy Question, as the prompt is asking you to comment on the current state of the law. Specifically, the purpose of the Policy Question is to give you, the student, an opportunity to:

* critique a certain law and its effects (i.e., on society, on the economy, on education, etc.),

* commend a certain law and its effects (i.e., on society, on the economy, on education, etc.),

* explain how a law should be created or changed to incentivize (or discourage) a certain behavior, and/or

* show how the law could be used to reach a particular societal or economic goal,

A couple of times in law school Part A of the exam was an Issue Spotter, and Part B was a Policy Question. It is difficult to give a specific example of a Policy Question and an exemplar response, as there are literally thousands of ways in which a policy question could be asked. Every student will have his/her own background knowledge, opinion, understanding, and even personal interaction with the law that they will bring into their response. Just know that if no fact pattern is provided, and the exam prompt in some way asks you to comment on a certain law, area of the law, or regulation, the exam is more than likely a Policy Question. If the professor does not give you specific instructions on what she is looking for in your response, at least do the following three things:

1) Briefly show what you know about the law.

In responding to a policy question, you probably won't need to IRAC anything, but if space allows, you may want to show the professor that you do have an understanding of the law. One way to do this is to analyze the law. For instance, if the prompt asks you to comment on rape law, you could briefly state the rule for rape, then comment on each element* of the crime. (*This is jumping ahead into Chapter 9, but think of an element of a crime like an ingredient. For a crime to be "rape," "murder," or whatever, there are certain ingredients, or elements, that must be present.) If you choose to carry out this step, keep it short, simple, and to the point. After all, the majority of a policy question response should be to comment on the law and offer suggestions for what the law ***should*** be, not what it is.

2) Bring in outside knowledge.

Draw on information you learned during your undergraduate studies or career. For instance, your background knowledge could offer the foundation of the argument or commentary presented in your response, or you could use your background knowledge to comment on the specified law or regulation.

You can also make mention of the historical, political, or cultural context of the law (and/or of current events) to help craft your policy response of what the law should be.

3) Provide your opinion.

Use what you know about the law and your background knowledge to offer your opinion of what the law should be. Relax. Enjoy it. Typically, there are no "wrong answers" to a policy question, so write away.

The Structure of a Response to a Policy Question

◇◇◇◇◇◇◇

There is no standard structure to answer a policy question. It depends on the course, your professor, and the question prompt. However, if you are struggling with how to begin or structure a response to a Policy Question Exam, both the Quote and Comment Method (Chapter 1) and the Observe and Cite Method (Chapter 2) can be used to answer a law school policy question. Refer to those chapters for an in-depth explanation, but here are the basics as they pertain to a policy question:

> Note: If you already have a structure in your mind of how to frame the response to the policy question, then please go with that. This section is only to provide some guidance to those who have absolutely no sense of where to start. In my experience, a Policy Question Exam is an opportunity for you to express yourself and interact with the law in your own unique way. If you feel stifled by the following structures, then please, answer the policy question your way.

Quote and Comment

◇◇◇◇◇◇◇

Here, your "quotes" will be the law, regulation, or policy suggestion. Remember, it doesn't necessarily have to be a direct quote, as a statement of the rule will suffice. Then, add in your commentary after each quote. Your commentary should respond to the "quote" using outside knowledge, your educational or career background, or your opinion.

Also, your commentary could provide your opinion of what the law should be. Your opinion should be based on something concrete, however, such as literature you have read, outside knowledge, your educational or career background, etc.

Lastly, your commentary could be how this law reminds you of another law, regulation, etc. Draw comparisons (and/or contrasts) between the two sources of law based on historical, political, or cultural context. Example plan:

I. Quote #1

— Commentary

II. Quote #2

— Commentary

III. Quote #3

— Commentary

> The "quotes" may be a statement of a law or regulation, a statement/explanation of a certain policy, or a quote of someone commenting on a certain law or policy.

Include as many commentaries as necessary to answer the policy question and/or thoroughly explain what you think the law or policy should be.

Observe and Cite

When you use the Observe and Cite structure to answer a policy question, the "observation" portion of your response will be your observation of how the law should be, and your "cite" will be your background knowledge (from undergraduate studies, career, outside literature, other disciplines, etc.) that back up your observation. Note that for the "cite" portion, a formal citation is not necessary for a policy question exam, especially if it's an in-class exam. In the context of responding to a law school policy question, "cite" means to make mention of your background knowledge. Example plan:

I. Observation #1: Change is needed because ...

- Cite: Background information of the law (historical, social, economic, etc. context of the law)

II. Observation #2: The law should be ...

- Cite: Outside, interdisciplinary knowledge.

III. Observation #3: It could be implemented by ...

- Cite: Background information, personal experience, interdisciplinary information, etc.

IV. Observation #4: The authorities should create awareness of the new policy by...

- Cite: Current events, change in culture, etc.

Include as many observations as necessary to answer the policy question and/or explain what the law should be. Also, include as many cites under each observation as necessary to introduce your own outside knowledge to help explain what the law should be.

Whether you choose to answer the policy question with the Quote and Comment, Observe and Cite, or your own method, don't forget to open with an engaging introduction (Chapter 4), close with a solid conclusion (Chapter 5), and to throw in a However Paragraph (Chapter 3) in your response. All are considered superfluous and unnecessary with an Issue Spotter Exam, but they bring depth to the policy paper.

Example Policy Paper Prompts

- *If you could change one law in the area of tort law, what would it be?* (It goes without saying, when responding to this type of question, you should explain why you would change that law and how you would change it.)
- *You are chosen to serve on the school advisory board to address a recent uptick in the number of reported rape allegations. Create an anti-rape policy that decreases the chances of a rape incident occurring and shows that the school is taking such cases/incidents seriously.*
- *Comment on any area of law we have covered in this class.*

One final note on policy papers

Do not be afraid to think out of the box. Often times, the professor is interested in hearing your unique perspective and novel ideas to the issue presented.

Chapter 9

◇◇◇◇◇

Legal Research

Law school is a professional school, and its purpose is to teach the profession of lawyering. As a lawyer, one of the assignments you will probably be tasked with is to draft a memorandum (typically to a partner or supervising attorney) that answers the question, "What does the law say, and how would it be applied in our client's case?"[1] Or, you may have to write a legal report (referred to as a "brief") to a court or judge explaining why a your client should prevail or how the court should rule. However, before you can complete either of the above two assignments, you must first do the legal research to find out what the law says.

So, in comes Legal Research and Writing.

The name of the course is different according to each law school, but Legal Research and Writing is the course that teaches you 1) how to do legal research, 2) how to write a memo (based on the legal research), and how to write a legal brief (also based on the legal research).

---

[1] That is, if you are a litigation attorney. There are two principal types of lawyers: litigation and transactional. Litigation attorneys are those most people usually think about when they hear "lawyer": completing lots of legal research, drafting motions, representing clients in court, etc. Transactional attorneys do work primarily concerned with business transactions such as drafting and reviewing contracts, creating legal business entities, completing and filing legal and tax forms, drafting wills, and reviewing business transactions (after the transaction has taken place) to make sure the legalities are in order. Transactional attorneys do not spend as much time in a courtroom as a litigation attorney.

The remainder of Chapter 9 provides guidelines for completing the initial legal research; Chapter 10 focuses on how to write a legal memo, and Chapter 11 covers the basics of how to approach a legal brief.

Legal research is simply finding out what the law says about a certain topic. Even more straightforward, in order to write a legal memo or legal brief, you first need to know the rules. What does the law say? The following chapter provides three practical routes to help find out what the law is:

1. Secondary Sources
2. Statutes, Regulations, and Codes
3. Case Law

Before we jump into the three main areas of legal research, it is necessary to note that the principal search engines used to do legal research are Westlaw and Lexis. Most lawyers and law students tend to prefer one over the other, but the preference is personal. (For me, the preference was arbitrary. I was introduced to one of them first... literally a few seconds before the other, so that is the one I gained comfort with.) However, it is wise to be able to navigate both Westlaw and Lexis, because sometimes you can find a case on one engine that did not show up on the other.

1) Secondary Sources (secondary authority)

Secondary sources, more often referred to as "secondary authority" in the legal profession, explain, comment on, and/or provide summaries of the law for a given topic. Examples of secondary authority are legal encyclopedias, legal treatises, law review articles, legal journals, and reports. Reading secondary authorities is helpful if you want to first gain a general overview of your assigned topic. If you decide to do such background reading, I suggest not spending more than one hour doing so, as you will want to focus most of your time on finding the actual cases you need to complete your legal memo or brief. Again, the main purpose of reading secondary authorities is to help you understand the topic by first getting a birds-eye view.

Another benefit of using secondary authority as the starting point of your research is that secondary authorities often reference statutes and case law that will come in handy later during your research.

There are many, many secondary sources/authorities. For instance, in Westlaw, if you click "Secondary Sources," a long list will pop up. However, if I were to review every secondary source, it would be overwhelming, and honestly, I did not discover some secondary sources until well into my third year of law school. (And some others I didn't even come across until *after* I had passed the bar.) Your knowledge of how to navigate the many resources offered by Westlaw and Lexis will increase as you grow as a law student and lawyer because your need for such resources will increase. As a 1L, however, you don't need to know everything about Westlaw or Lexis; you just need to know enough to get you through your legal memo and/or brief. Just stick with the basics. Hence, the two basic secondary resources that will be most helpful to you in your first year of law school are legal encyclopedias and law reviews/journals.

* **Legal Encyclopedias** are grouped by topic (i.e., Criminal Law, Family Law, Torts, etc.) and provide helpful summaries of different areas of the law. Legal encyclopedias are the most helpful secondary source for someone who simply wants a quick understanding of the law. Personally, I most frequently used the *American Law Reports*. Another popular, helpful secondary source was *American Jurisprudence*. Once you choose a legal encyclopedia, treatise, etc., next choose the area of law (i.e., Criminal, Family, etc.) that is pertinent to your assignment. Then, type in the relevant search terms into the search box. A list of articles will populate. After reviewing the most relevant articles, you should have enough background knowledge to understand the law and move forward in your research.

  For instance, let's say the assignment is to draft a memo explaining whether or not the client has a viable claim for negligent infliction of emotional distress. To complete the background research, first, filter your preferred search engine (WestLaw or Lexis) for American Law Reports (or any legal encyclopedia) regarding Tort Law. Enter the following into the search box: "negligent infliction of emotional distress." Finally, spend a few minutes getting abreast of the information before moving on to finding the case law.

* **Law Reviews and Journals** are helpful for those who want to read on specific, niche areas of the law. Whereas the American Law Reports (ALRs) provide excellent overviews of topics, law reviews and journal articles tend to provide the overview at the beginning of the article, but then the remainder of the article is dedicated to an analysis, critique, or unexplored effect or niche of the law. As a 1L who just wants to get a basic understanding, the analysis/critique portion of the article(s) may overwhelm you. Thus, I suggest 1Ls stick to the ALRs for background knowledge.

To complete research using law reviews or journal articles:

1. Search for law review or journal articles from Westlaw or Lexis by going to the law review and/or journal section.

2. Filter your selection by journal name (if you know it), or more generally by topic.
3. Then, enter search terms relevant to your topic.

2) Statutes, Regulations, and Codes (primary authority)

Primary sources of the law are the document, book, or other publication wherein the rules are codified or written. Primary sources of the law are most often referred to as "primary authority" in the legal profession and may include items such as the Constitution, an actual statute and/or regulation, and case opinions. (When the original source of the law is a case, this is called, "case law." How to find case law is the focus of the next subsection.)

When I was a law student, the text of the statute was provided in the memo assignment. However, if your school does not provide the original text of the statute, regulation, or code, but you want to read it, you can search for it in Westlaw or Lexis. Your search will depend on what information you are starting with. First off, an ALR article (explained on the previous page, under "Legal Encyclopedias") may include the text of the law, or at least make mention of where it has been codified. Or, if you have a portion of the actual text of the statute, then begin your Westlaw or Lexis search by setting the filter for "regulations, codes, or statutes" (the precise filter depends on the search engine). Then enter, in quotations, as a direct-quote, the text from the regulation into the search box.

Alternatively, if you have the name or citation of the statute, then you can enter that into the search box (after setting the search filters to the best of your ability). This final method (searching the citation of the statute) is a bit tricky because, depending on your filters, the search engine will probably populate a bunch of places where the statute has been mentioned. Don't be afraid to click around (in Westlaw or Lexis) until you find what you are looking for. Even more importantly, don't be afraid to ask a librarian. As a 1L, I had countless meetings with the law librarians.

3) Case Law (primary authority)

Case law is another type of primary authority. Although sometimes you will need to research statutes and regulations, most times, you will need to research the law by finding cases that established a certain law, also known as case precedent. Hence, researching the case law means researching the legal rule as defined by a case. Sometimes the rule is clearly stated, and you don't have to do much work other than read the case and find the rule statement. Other times, however, the rule is embedded within the discussion of the case, and you will have to piece together the rule statement. Alternatively, if it is simply not possible to create a rule statement, you may have to argue generally that your case is similar (or dissimilar, if you want a different outcome for your client) to the facts of the case precedent.

How To Find What You Need

◇◇◇◇◇◇◇

Now that you have a general idea of the different big "areas" of legal research, here are some guidelines to help you find the information that you need to write your legal memo or brief. Much of the following pertains to finding case law, as you'll spend the majority of your time looking for case law. However, you can also use the following guidelines when looking for background information and/or primary sources.

- **Breathe.** You will get through this. Honestly, I found a lot of information and cases by trial and error and by clicking around Westlaw and Lexis. This writing guide, your instructor, and a law librarian are here to help you ease frustration.

- **Jurisdiction:** Make sure that when you begin to search for cases, you set your filters to the correct jurisdiction. Your assignment materials should state the jurisdiction of your fictional case. Ideally, you want to find cases within the specific jurisdiction provided in your assignment materials. However, if you cannot find a case within the *exact* jurisdiction specified in your assignment materials, it is ok to use a case from a higher court. This can get confusing, but the following diagram of the hierarchy of the legal system should make it clear.

> Note: The following is a very basic, very "bare-bones" diagram of the U.S. court system. It does not include every type of court. Instead, it includes those courts you will likely be researching and citing to in your first year of law school.

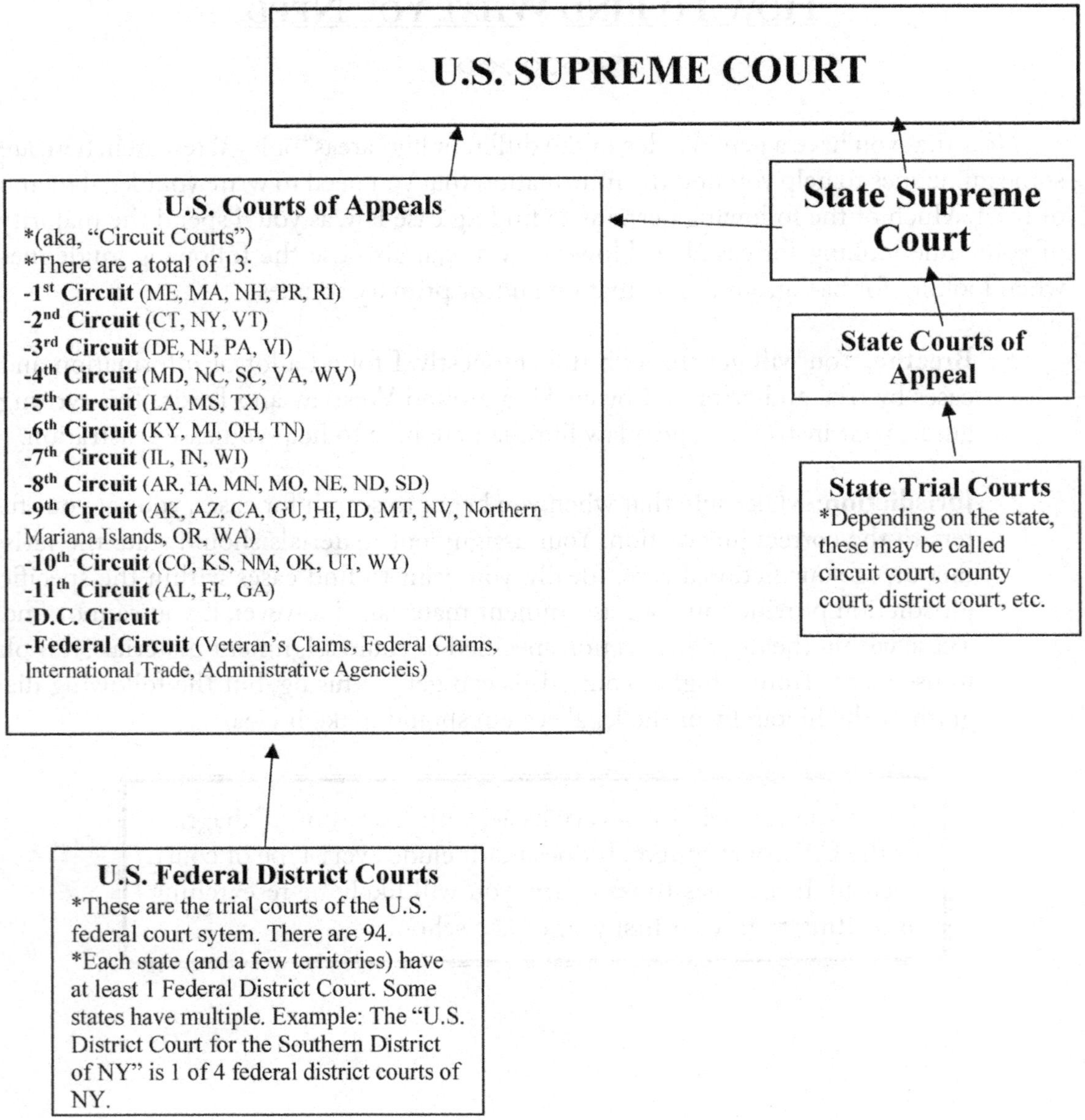
U.S. SUPREME COURT
U.S. Courts of Appeals
*(aka, "Circuit Courts")
*There are a total of 13:
-1st Circuit (ME, MA, NH, PR, RI)
-2nd Circuit (CT, NY, VT)
-3rd Circuit (DE, NJ, PA, VI)
-4th Circuit (MD, NC, SC, VA, WV)
-5th Circuit (LA, MS, TX)
-6th Circuit (KY, MI, OH, TN)
-7th Circuit (IL, IN, WI)
-8th Circuit (AR, IA, MN, MO, NE, ND, SD)
-9th Circuit (AK, AZ, CA, GU, HI, ID, MT, NV, Northern Mariana Islands, OR, WA)
-10th Circuit (CO, KS, NM, OK, UT, WY)
-11th Circuit (AL, FL, GA)
-D.C. Circuit
-Federal Circuit (Veteran's Claims, Federal Claims, International Trade, Administrative Agencieis)
State Supreme Court
State Courts of Appeal
State Trial Courts
*Depending on the state, these may be called circuit court, county court, district court, etc.
U.S. Federal District Courts
*These are the trial courts of the U.S. federal court sytem. There are 94.
*Each state (and a few territories) have at least 1 Federal District Court. Some states have multiple. Example: The "U.S. District Court for the Southern District of NY" is 1 of 4 federal district courts of NY.

The State System (right side of diagram)

So, for instance, if the assignment states that the case will be brought in a Florida District Court, you first want to find cases from one of the Florida District Courts. However, unless the assignment advises otherwise, it is acceptable to use a case from one of the Florida courts of appeal or from the Florida Supreme Court.

On the other hand, if your client's case is being brought in a Florida District Court, it would **not** be wise to use a case from, for instance, a Minnesota District Court or from the Minnesota Supreme Court.

The Federal System (left side of diagram)

Let's say, for example, the assignment states that the case will be brought in a Louisiana *Federal* District Court, then ideally, you want to find cases from that particular Louisiana Federal District Court. However, you can also include cases (into your memo or brief) from the U.S. Court of Appeals for the 5th Circuit.

Also, note that in this example, Louisiana has 3 Federal District Courts:

* Eastern District of Louisiana (federal)

* Western District of Louisiana (federal)

* Middle District of Louisiana (federal)

Ideally, you want cases from the exact federal court wherein your client's case will be heard. However, if you cannot find a case in the exact federal court wherein your case will be litigated, it is generally acceptable to use cases from one of the other Louisiana Federal District Courts. Double-check with your instructor or supervisor. Of course, it is also acceptable to use cases from the U.S. Supreme Court, since it is the highest court of the land.

Search for case law by typing in the exact legal phrase in quotations.

Your law school assignment (or instructor) should make it clear what that legal phrase is. You will become familiar with legal phrases and what to search as you progress as a law student and attorney. Furthermore, your supervisor will usually tell you what she is looking for. Quotations are important at this phase of the research process because they hone in your results. Example(s):

"negligent infliction of emotional distress"

"discretionary function"
"intentional infliction of emotional distress"
"insanity defense"

Synonyms

You can also find cases by entering synonyms or phrases that are interchangeable with the legal phrase you initially searched for. Again, your familiarity with legal phrases will grow as you progress as a law student and attorney. Example(s):

For a manslaughter case, the following search terms could be used:

"unintentional homicide"
"2nd degree murder"
"second degree murder"
"unintentional murder"
"unintentional killing"

Word Variations and Stretching

Use variations of the word you are using by "stretching" (or truncating) the root of the word or phrase. Example(s):

For *rob*, also search *robber* and *robbery*.
For *liability*, also search *liable*.

Connectors

Use connectors to give the search engine specific directions on how to treat your search terms. Using connectors will help the search engine generate cases that are specific and relevant to your topic. Do not stress yourself out by trying to concoct the most superior search algorithm. Instead, the above guidelines, coupled with the following, basic commands should help you find the cases you need.

" " Quotation marks make sure your search results only include the specific phrase contained within the quotation marks.

and Tells the search engine to return results where both of the search terms are present in the case, document, etc. Example: the search command [infancy and juvenile] will populate results where the words *infancy* and *juvenile* are both mentioned in the same case or document.

or Tells the search engine to return results where any of the search terms are mentioned. You don't have to type in "or," as it can be represented by a space. For example, a search of [attorney medic physician] will populate results wherein *attorney, medic*, or *physician* is mentioned. Each document or case that populates may not mention all three terms, but each document/case will have at least one of those terms mentioned in it.

! Put an (!) at the end of the search term to gather cases that include the root of the word. Example(s):

Jurisdiction! would yield cases that include the word *jurisdiction, jurisdictions, jurisdictional,* etc.

Liab! would yield cases that include *liability, liable,* etc.

/s Use (/s) to connect search terms. Specifically, /s means "these terms must be in the same sentence." For example, if you enter "federal /s jurisdiction," you are telling the search engine to give you cases where *federal* is used within the same sentence as *jurisdiction*.

/3 means "these terms must be within 3 words of each other." For example, if you enter, [murder /3 insanity], you are telling the search engine to give you cases where *murder* is mentioned within 3 words of *insanity*.

/p means "these terms must be within the same paragraph." For example, if you enter, ["illegal substance" /p "poisonous tree"], you are telling the search engine to give you cases where the phrase *illegal substance* is mentioned within the same paragraph as *poisonous tree*.

Combine connectors to find what you need. For instance, the search [arrest! /2 "illegal detention"] will yield results where any word with the root of *arrest* is within two words of the phrase *illegal detention*.

Look to your memo/brief assignment for direction and clues on search terms.

For instance, if the assignment is about the negligent infliction of emotional distress, then you would start your legal research by first making sure you are in the correct jurisdiction, then entering "negligent infliction of emotional distress" into the search box. After reviewing the cases that populate from that first search, the next search term to enter could be "NIED," which is the abbreviation for "negligent infliction of emotional distress." (I just happen to know that sometimes legal texts and cases refer to that particular tort by its abbreviation, so that is why I knew to search for it by the initials. As you read more and more legal texts, you will become familiar with legal jargon and what terms to search. However, if you're new to legal research, do not be afraid to ask your law librarian for help with synonyms to search for.)

Ask for help.

If it gets unbearably too hard and you've been searching for one case for hours on end, ask the law librarian. Doing so does not make you a failure. In fact, you may be hitting the same roadblock that your former law school peers are running up against. During my first semester of law school, I remember searching for a case for over five hours! (Over two to three days or so, I would search, get frustrated, walk away, then come back and search some more.) I can laugh at this now, but I remember feeling so frustrated and defeated at the time that the assignment brought me to tears. Finally, my roommate and I talked about it, and she shared with me, "Yeah, I couldn't figure out that part of the memo either. I went and got help from the librarian, and he was saying that there's usually a difficult one to find. He helped me through it, though." Needless to say, I found myself meeting with a librarian the next day. So, you never know, you might be hitting a roadblock in your research because you are supposed to. Instead of beating yourself up about it and continuing to wander around in research circles, get help from the research experts – the law librarians. Alternatively, you could also ask your instructor or the class teaching assistant for help.

Organize your research as you research.

Doing so will save you lots of time and frustration, and you'll be able to focus your energy on writing a well-written analysis, as opposed to wasting precious hours looking for that one case that discussed that one thing that you remember reading but just can't remember where it's at. (Clearly, I have been a victim of such frustration.) So, for instance, if you are looking for cases that list the elements of murder, then write "Elements of First

Degree Murder," across the top of your paper before you begin to list all the pertinent cases. Next, if you are looking for cases that define, *specifically*, the premeditation requirement of first-degree murder, entitle the next list "Premeditation," then list all the cases you will use to analyze premeditation. Next, if you are looking for cases that specifically discuss the requirement that first-degree murder be intentional, entitle this list of research notes as "Intentionality," before you start jotting down all the cases you've found.

Also, be sure to jot down the full citation of the case in your research notes. Nothing is more annoying than to know you have the perfect case with the perfect rule statement, only to find that you only listed "Smith v. Jones" in your research notes, and there are a million "Smith v. Jones" cases in Lexis/Westlaw.

If you prefer not to write (or type) your research notes, Lexis and Westlaw both have features to save your research to folders, so that is another way you can stay organized while researching.

Read the case headings as you research.

Both Westlaw and Lexis provide headings at the beginning of the cases. The heading is a summary of the case, so as you research, read the headings to get an idea of the facts and the major legal issues of the case. Doing so will allow you to quickly decide whether or not the case is useful. Also, the heading blurbs are hyperlinked, such that when you click on the hyperlink, you can drop down to where that issue is discussed in the case. The hyperlinked blurbs are also helpful to find other cases that discuss the same issue.

As you find cases, you will notice that some cases re-state the same rule.

Once you have found the rule statement you need, there is no need to read *every* case with the same rule statement. In your memo or brief, just cite to one or two cases that state the pertinent rule. Regarding those "extra" cases (i.e., they are extra because they're just re-stating the rule statement you've already found in other cases), still save those cases. You might be able to use them later, not for that particular rule, but for the discussion and analysis sections of your memo or brief.

How do you know when you are done researching a certain topic?

Regarding background research, you are done researching secondary sources once you have a general understanding of the law. Regarding case law research, you are done researching when the rule statements you find (from the cases) are simply echoing themselves; when you are no longer finding anything new.

Cross-reference your research findings.

After you do your search in one search engine (Westlaw or Lexis), don't forget to check out the other. Sometimes one of the search engines will pick up a case that the other does not.

Before you submit your memo or brief, be sure to check if the cases you have cited to have been reversed, overruled, or overturned.

If a case has been reversed or overturned, it is now "bad law." You don't want bad law in your memo or brief, as you want to make sure your analysis is based on current law. Westlaw refers to this process as "Keycite." In Westlaw, a red flag indicates "Trouble! There is a high chance that something in here is bad law." A yellow flag indicates "Warning. Be careful." Lexis refers to it as *Shepardize*. In Lexis, you will see a red (or yellow) dot, followed by a warning message.

However, just because you see a warning sign does not mean you have to throw the case out. Oftentimes, a case includes many legal issues, and sometimes, the part of the case that was overturned is not relevant to your analysis, or why you used the case. So, even if there is a red or yellow warning sign, be sure to read the case to make sure the "bad law" that the system is warning you about actually has anything to do with the legal issue, rule statement, or whatever you were using the case for.

CHAPTER 10

◇◇◇◇◇

THE LEGAL MEMO

The purpose of the legal memo is for you to answer the question, "What does the law say about this situation?" When you take into account the different areas of law, I'm sure there are millions of permutations of this question, but for instance, you may be asked to explain:

- a particular regulation and how it applies to your client, **OR**

- the likely outcome for your client based on how the court has decided a similar issue (i.e., based on "case precedent" or "case law"), **OR**

- whether or not you can file a certain case in a certain court, **OR**

- what defenses are at your client's disposal… **OR**

- a plethora of other questions that require legal research.

CLOSED MEMO VS. OPEN MEMO

◇◇◇◇◇◇◇

At Harvard Law School, there were two big memo assignments: the closed memo and the open memo. The closed memo was "closed" because the legal research had been done for us. As if we were starting off with training wheels, we were given seven to eight cases (which contained the pertinent legal rules), and our only responsibility was to use those cases to explain to the fictitious supervising attorney how the law applied to our client. Then came the open memo assignment, where we had to complete the legal research and find the cases ourselves, plus write the memo.

I remember when I first received the closed memo assignment as a 1L. Each of the seven cases was only about eight pages in length. Although I had listened attentively to the in-class lecture, and I knew my job was to figure out how the legal precedent applied to the facts provided in our fictitious case, I didn't know where to start. Overwhelmed by the intimidating responsibility to write a legal analysis in my second week of law school, I headed home to take the approach I had always taken when it came to academics: dive right in. Then, another 1L approached me, and before long, the topic of discussion turned to the closed memo:

"Well," she offered, "A 2L told me that all you have to do is use the cases that work to your advantage."

Ahh! I thought. *What a load off. I don't have to read, much less analyze, all the cases they gave us. I'll just use the ones with the outcome I need.*

WRONG!

Before we move any further with instructions on how to draft a legal memo, I must caution you that it is not wise to ignore cases that do not work to your fictitious client's advantage, especially if you are completing a closed memo assignment. First, in the context of a closed memo, they (the course instructors) have done the work for you by giving you the cases to use. Since they have given you everything you need, use it up! Second, speaking more generally (i.e., in the real world), unless the assigning attorney has given you other precise directions, they should know as much as possible about the legal rule, regulation, etc., they've asked you about, even if it is not in the client's favor. You can still learn something about the legal rule from those cases where the outcome is not favorable to the client. This doesn't mean to include an analysis of *every* case that is not in your client's favor, as you would have a never-ending memo if you did so. However, if there has been a recent decision that has significant implications for the client, be sure to mention it in the legal memo, even if it is not in your client's favor, and explain how that decision might affect the client. Note that, unless the assignment or supervising attorney says differently, the purpose of a legal memo is not to persuade; the purpose is to inform. Hence, for the legal memo, (unless the assignment or supervising attorney instructs differently) you do not want to try to "twist" the law to work in the client's favor. The brief (covered in Chapter 11) will be more geared towards persuasion.

HOW TO APPROACH A LEGAL MEMO

◇◇◇◇◇◇◇◇

Typically, there will be a particular law, legal issue, or regulation that the fictitious supervising attorney asks you about. From a bird's-eye view, your job is to explain what the law is, apply the law to the facts provided, and offer a plausible, likely conclusion based on the law.

Now, to get into the weeds a bit: First, find the case with a rule statement that provides a clear definition of the particular law or regulation being asked about. Typically, the definition will include different elements that must first be decided upon and weighed before a final conclusion can be reached. For instance, say the supervising attorney asks, "What does the case law say about a good law student? Do you think a court would consider our client a good law student?" To begin, you need to find a case (if it's a closed memo, then the case will be provided to you) that gives a rule stating the definition of a **good law student**. Say the case states the following: "In order to be considered a good law student, one must be enrolled in an ABA-accredited institution, complete all the readings, never miss class, and give it their best shot." Based on the rule statement, there are four elements, or requirements, to being a good law student:

1. Enrollment in an ABA-accredited law school,
2. Completion of all the readings,
3. Perfect attendance, and
4. Giving it their best shot.

You will now spend the majority of the memo on each element of the law: summarizing cases that define each element, and then applying the rule for each element to the facts of your fictitious case. I know this sounds complicated, but I promise it is not. *If you know the formula.* I provide the formula and examples in the following pages. Also, it was helpful for me to look at the structure of a legal memo. Each law school, partner, or supervising has their own expectations, but so you have an idea of what a memo looks like, here is a general outline:

I. Heading
II. Question Presented
III. Brief Answer
IV. Facts
V. Discussion
VI. Conclusion

I. Heading

Include the name of the partner or supervising attorney, author, subject of memo, and the date. Typically located at the top, on the left, of the first page of the memo. Example:

> To: Jane M. Bolin, Esq.
> From: New Assistant U.S. Attorney
> Date: February 15, 2018
> Re: Rodriguez v. United States - Good Law Student

II. Question Presented

A simple, brief restatement of the legal question posed by the supervising attorney. State the parties involved, the main facts, the cause of action or legal category, and the precise legal issue. Example:

> Can we successfully present the "good law student defense" for Imani, who has a 3.57 law school grade point average and has missed a total of four classes since beginning law school?

III. Brief Answer

Briefly answer the question presented. A one-word sentence will do (i.e., "Yes." or "Probably not."), followed by a summary of the legal rule (also called the "legal doctrine") and an application of the general legal doctrine to the facts. Example:

> Yes. Pursuant to the Federal Guidelines of Student Conduct, law students can avoid all tort and criminal liability if they are deemed a good law student. Imani has been a full-time student at the University of Alabama School of Law for the past two years; she completes a majority of the reading assignments; and she has consistently given her best effort at assignments, projects, and exams. Although Imani has missed a few classes, the weight of the other factors is likely to lead the court to conclude that Imani is a good student.

IV. Facts

Include all the factual information necessary to resolve the legal problem. Make sure the Facts section includes all the facts that you mention in the Discussion section. In law school, you will probably also be expected to include background information and the procedural history of the case.

Present the facts from a fair, objective viewpoint. You should only be narrating what happened, not trying to persuade.

Also, even if the assignment requires that you gather the facts from multiple sources, organize the facts in a way that is easy to understand, which typically turns out to be chronologically.

EXAMPLE

Imani Rodriguez is currently a 3L at the University of Alabama School of Law. She accepted an admission offer in March 2015 and enrolled in law school on August 20, 2015. She has been registered as a full-time law student throughout the entirety of her law school tenure. Also, affidavits from her professors indicate that she is an attentive student who regularly attends class. Her class schedule, which was issued on the official letterhead from the University of Alabama School of Law, shows that she is currently enrolled in four classes.

On September 1, 2016, she was involved in a serious car accident. As a result of the accident, a number of tort actions have been filed against her. However, at the time of the accident, as well as currently, she is a full-time law student at the University of Alabama School of Law, which is an ABA-accredited law school. During Imani's first visit to our office, she revealed that she does not always complete all of the assigned reading. When pressed to give an estimate of the percentage of the readings she completes, Imani responded, "Definitely more than half. I would say 70%, but when I don't get to a reading, I always review the pertinent section of the course outline or a classmate's notes." She also explained that she had never missed a day of class until the car accident. However, as a result of the accident she has missed a total of four lectures to attend medical and legal appointments. Whenever she misses a class, she reviews an outline or notes from a classmate, she regularly attends office hours, takes multiple practice exams for each class, and has maintained a 3.57 grade point average. Imani also serves as the executive editor for the Public Policy Journal, and she is the co-chair for the school's award-winning mock trial team.

V. Discussion

The discussion section is the main entrée of your legal memo. This is where you complete the legal analysis by stating the legal rules and applying that doctrine to the facts. In terms of space, the discussion section will take up most of your memo. The following explains how to write the Discussion by providing formulas to complete an effective analysis. An example, that models the formulas, is provided afterwards.

I was taught a specific formula to complete case analyses in legal memos: "CRuPAC," pronounced *crew-pack.*

CRuPAC

Conclusion
Rule
Proof
Application
Conclusion

CONCLUSION – State the conclusion. By applying the law to the provided facts, clearly state how the case at hand is likely to turn out.

RULE – State the rule. This is taken from the case(s) you found while researching. Sometimes the rule is given explicitly in a case. Other times, however, you will have to create a rule statement using a case (or multiple cases) from your research.

PROOF – State the relevant authority for the rule. Typically, this is simply the citation of a case, statute, regulation, or policy. ("Authority" is the fancy legal word for case, statute, regulation, or policy. It answers the question, "Says who?")

– Also, be sure to include any counter authorities (i.e., cases that counter the rule/law of this particular CRuPAC). Mention the counter-authorities by including a "*but see,*" followed by the contrary authority. If you choose to mention any counter authority, see the following Application/Analysis section for instruction on how to deal with the counter authority.

APPLICATION (OR "ANALYSIS") – Apply the rule to the facts at hand. That is, how does the law interact with the facts of your case?

– **Compare:** An effective method of analysis is to compare the facts of the case precedent to the facts of the case at hand. To make this as neat and precise as possible, first, give the background facts of the case precedent, then use one (or some) of these formulas to craft a precise comparison between the facts of the case precedent and the facts of the case at hand:

- Like the defendant (or plaintiff) in *Smith v. State*, who ____________, our client also [insert comparative action].
- Similar to *US vs. Gray*, where ________________, in the case at hand [insert the fact you are comparing].
- Like the [hospital/doctor/student/employee etc.] in *Topey v. Williams*, which/who [insert pertinent fact], in the case at hand, [insert name of comparative hospital/doctor/student/employee, etc.] (+) [insert comparative action or conduct].

– **Contrast:** If you want to argue that your case should come out differently than the case precedent: First, give the background facts of the case precedent, then try one (or some) of these constructions to *contrast* the facts of the case precedent against the facts of the case at hand:

- Unlike the defendant (or plaintiff) in *Smith v. State*, who ____________, our client [insert contrasting action/conduct].

- Whereas in *US vs. Gray*, [insert fact, conduct, or action], in the case at hand [insert the fact you are contrasting].

- Unlike the [hospital/doctor/student/employee etc.] in *Topey v. Williams*, which/who [insert pertinent fact], in the case at hand, [insert name of contrasting hospital/doctor/student/employee, etc.] (+) [insert contrasting action or conduct].

– **Policy arguments:** When relevant, you can also conduct your analysis by giving reasoning based on policy. What sound policy would result from the application (or non-application) of the law/rule to the facts at hand? That is, you can use this section to reason that the law/rule should be applied a certain way to encourage (or discourage) certain conduct. Note, however, that policy arguments are not always welcome in legal memos. Be sure to read the instructions carefully or check-in with the course instructor (or in a real-life situation, with the supervising attorney).

– **Regarding counter-authorities:** If you mentioned a counter-authority in the Proof section, then address that counter-authority in the Analysis/Application section:

1. Give a brief summary of that case (facts and the doctrine).
2. Contrast the counter-authority with the facts of the case at hand.
3. Explain why you are not using the outcome/legal rule in the counter-authority as precedent for the case at hand.

CONCLUSION – Recap your conclusion in one sentence.

Discussion Section Example

◇◇◇◇◇◇◇◇

Begin the discussion section with a thesis statement. That is, begin with a general CRuPAC that states the general doctrine and applies it, generally, to the facts. (This is typically 1-2 sentences.) Then, use the remainder of the discussion to complete CRuPACs for each element of the legal rule.

Thesis: Begin with a general CRuPAC.

◇◇◇◇◇◇◇◇

Conclusion

Imani is a good law student. A good law student is an individual who is enrolled in an ABA-accredited school, completes all law school readings, never misses class, and gives it their best shot. *Law School vs. The People*, 477 U.S. 33 (2018). "The absence of one factor, alone, does not preclude an individual from being a good law student." *The State vs. High Achievers*, 98 F.3d 23, 28 (2018). All factors must be weighed. *Id.* Imani Tisdale is currently taking classes at The University of Alabama School of Law. She reads most of the assigned cases and reviews notes for the reading she is unable to complete. She has a good attendance record, and her academic consistency and extracurricular involvement show that she has been giving her best effort at having a successful law school experience. A judge is likely to find that Imani is a good law student.

Rule

Proof

Proof

Notice: There is no need to re-write the full case citation again. "Id." means "The authority for this statement is the same authority that was just cited to."

Application/ Analysis

Conclusion

> Notice: the "rule" of the CruPAC for the Thesis section was not one rule statement. Instead, rule statements from two, different cases were pieced together to adequately address the issue. Sometimes, you will need to piece together the rule from multiple cases.

PART 1 – CRuPAC ELEMENT 1.

◇◇◇◇◇◇◇◇

Conclusion

Imani is enrolled in an ABA-accredited law school. An individual is enrolled in an ABA-accredited law school if they have accepted an offer of admission into an institution that is on the ABA-approved list of law schools, are registered as a part-time or full-time student at that school, and regularly attends classes according to a school-issued class schedule. *Student vs. Harvard Law School*, 98 U.S. 45 (2013). Imani accepted an offer of admission to the University of Alabama School of Law, which is on the ABA-approved list as an accredited institution. Her student history indicates that she has been registered as a full-time law student throughout law school. Her class schedule was issued by the school, as it includes an official school header displaying the school seal. The class schedule shows that she is currently enrolled in four law school classes, and the affidavits from the professor state that she regularly attend classes. Therefore, Imani is enrolled in an ABA-accredited law school.

Rule

Proof

Application/
Analysis

Conclusion

Part 2 – CRuPAC element 2.

◇◇◇◇◇◇◇

Imani does not complete all readings; nevertheless, she studies effectively. Completion of all the readings requires that a law student reads 100% of every word and footnote of every case, law review article, and regulation handbook assigned by the professor. *Gunner vs. The State*, 100 F.2d 24 (2014). "Completion of most of the main text of the assigned reading, coupled with consistent review of course outlines and class notes, give the same outcome as completion of all the readings." *Realist vs. Florida* 90 F.4d 90, 104 (2018). Since Imani does not always read 100% of every word and footnote of every case, law review article, and regulation handbook, she does not complete all of the readings according to *Gunner*. However, when Imani misses a class, she reviews the course outlines and notes taken by other students in the class. Hence, as outlined by *Realist v. Florida*, Imani's study habits give the same outcome as completion of all the readings. Although Imani does not complete all readings, her study habits are effective.

Part 3 – CRuPAC element 3.

◇◇◇◇◇◇◇

Imani does not have perfect attendance. A student has perfect attendance if they are present, physically or by pre-approved virtual means, at every class for all three years of school. *Battles vs. County School District*, 34 U.S. 16 (2014). Although Imani had never missed a day of class before the accident, she has missed four lectures as a result of the accident. Imani does not have perfect attendance.

> Notice that this rule statement does not specifically mention "law school student." Sometimes, you will have to explore other, yet similar and applicable, areas of the law to find a rule statement.

Part 4 – CRuPAC element 4.

◇◇◇◇◇◇◇

Imani gives law school her best shot. A student gives their best shot at law school if he/she makes a serious effort to "catch up" when she falls behind, attends office hours, prepares for exams, and is involved in extracurricular activities. *Angelo vs. Imposter Syndrome*, 98 F.6d 3 (2016). Imani reviews the daily class outline or notes from a classmate whenever she misses class, she regularly attends office hours, takes multiple practice exams for each class, and she holds leadership positions in two extracurricular activities: the Public Policy Journal and the mock trial team.

In *Wesson v. Administrative Board of Broader County,* the plaintiff, a second-year law student, argued that she gave law school her best shot. The *Wesson* plaintiff had admittedly missed over 75% of her law school classes, opting instead to watch Netflix during the semester and show up on exam day. The plaintiff in *Wesson* also never attended office hours. Nevertheless, she argued that because she took multiple practice exams for each class, consistently scored within the top 5% on all of her exams, and was an Editor for the Sports Law Review, that she gave law school her best shot. The court disagreed. It found that despite her exam scores and extracurricular involvement, she had not given law school her best effort because she skipped a significant amount of class time and never attended office hours. Unlike the plaintiff in *Wesson*, who never attended office hours, Imani regularly attends office hours. Also, whereas the *Wesson* plaintiff missed over half of her classes to watch Netflix, Imani has missed only four lectures, and she reviews an outline or class notes whenever she is absent from class. Therefore, a court is likely to find that Imani is giving law school her best shot.

> The above paragraph is an example of how to contrast the facts of another case against the facts of your client's case. You want to contrast the facts if you find a case with the rule statement you need, but you need a different outcome for your client.

VI. Conclusion (of the legal memo)

- State the brief answer to the question presented. Identify the most likely outcome based on how the law/rule would apply to the facts in your case. Note: It is typically not required to include ***both*** a "Brief Answer" and a "Conclusion" section in your memo. Check in with your instructor or supervising attorney to comply with their preferences.

EXAMPLE

The good law student defense is a viable defense for Imani. A good law student is an individual who is enrolled in an ABA-accredited school, completes all law school readings, never misses class, and gives it their best shot. *Law School vs. The People*, 477 U.S. 33 (2018). The absence of one factor, alone, is not dispositive of an individual's status as a good law student, as all the factors must be considered and balanced. *See The State vs. High Achievers*, 98 F.3d 23, 28 (2018). Although Imani falls short on some of the elements of a good law student, namely completing all the reading assignments and perfect attendance, the strength of the other factors sufficiently outweighs any shortcomings. Specifically, because Imani completes most of the law school readings and reviews the outlines and class notes when she is unable to complete the reading, has missed only four classes as a result of the accident, and gives law school her best shot, the court is likely to find that Imani is a good law student.

> Notice that *See* is added here, because this is not an exact statement of what was stated in the case. The exact statement (also provided in the Thesis example on p. 77) : "The absence of one factor, alone, does not preclude an individual from being a good law student."

Last-Minute Tips for the Legal Memo

◇◇◇◇◇◇◇

Regarding the "Facts" section:

- For an open memo assignment, the facts may come from various sources. For instance, I remember having to gather facts from (fake) evidence such as internal employee memos, depositions, photos, and even the case pleadings. Even if you have to gather the facts from various sources, make sure that you present them in an orderly, logical fashion in your memo. Chronological order, or presenting the events and information as they happened, tends to be the typical order in most memos, especially when completing a memo assignment for law school. On the other hand, in complex cases, organizing the facts thematically may make more sense. Unless you take a class like "Advanced Legal Research and Writing," you probably won't have to deal with complex cases/memos in law school. This is more likely to be seen in the real world of litigation.

- **Including the most pertinent facts:** First, write a generic Facts section to get started. Then, as you complete your CRuPACs, go back and edit the Facts session as necessary, adding facts you included in your analysis (i.e., in the CRuPACs), and omitting uneccessary facts (i.e., those you initially thought were necessary for the analysis that ended up not being so important).

Regarding the Discussion section:

- Divide your Discussion section into subsections by using informative headings. Doing so helps the reader to follow your analysis. Typically, the subheadings will correspond to the various parts of your analysis. For instance, subheadings for the Discussion section for the example case included in this chapter would have corresponded to the various elements of the good student defense:

  Enrollment in an ABA-accredited law school

  Completion of Readings

  Perfect Attendance

  Giving Her Best Shot

Under each subheading would be the CRuPAC for that particular element.

- Make sure you use controlling law. Choose cases that are most relevant and have the greatest precedential weight for your jurisdiction.

- Explain the court's reasoning in the controlling cases.

- Acknowledge and distinguish contrary authority or competing arguments. Present and evaluate counterarguments fairly. This does not mean you have to mention *every* potential argument for the other side. However, it is a good idea to identify and analyze the weight of contrary authority and/or bad facts (that is, facts that are not in your client's favor).

Chapter 11

The Legal Brief

"Brief" is the name of the document wherein the parties to a legal dispute that has been appealed to a higher court lay out their arguments before an appellate court. (FYI, "court" and "judge" are oftentimes used interchangeably in law school and the legal profession). Typically, both sides to the legal dispute will write a brief to the court that: summarizes the legal dispute and facts, lays out their argument, and asks the court to rule a certain way. Hence, whereas the legal memo (covered in Chapter 10) mainly focuses on objectively presenting the law and predicting how a court is likely to rule, briefs tend to be persuasive in nature. More often than not, the parties hire attorneys or law firms to create the arguments and write the brief on their behalf; hence, law students must learn how to write a legal brief. Note that this type of brief being discussed in this writing guide is different from case briefs. Whereas the type of brief covered here is referring to a document that lays out legal arguments and analyses before a judge, case briefs are summaries of the cases you read as part of a law school class.

Also, sometimes a non-profit, business, school, research organization, advocacy organization, or even a professional association that is not a party in the dispute wants to persuade the court to rule a certain way. If so, the organization will write an *amicus curiae* brief (colloquially referred to as an "amicus brief") that offers the court additional information that it should take into consideration in making its decision. *Amicus curiae* comes from the Latin phrase meaning "friend of the court." Of course, it is the court's discretion as to whether it will accept an amicus brief.

How to Approach a Brief

◇◇◇◇◇◇◇◇

The overall goal of the brief is to use case law (i.e. precedent), reasoning, and sometimes policy to persuade the judge to make a decision in your client's favor. Here are some step-by-step instructions to help you get started:

1) Get a grip. Find your bearings.

Whichever idiomatic expression you most identify with, just be sure to first take time to orient yourself with the case. To each his own, but it may be helpful to take notes during this phase of the process. Even if your notes are scattered all over the place and seem nonsensical, as you move forward with developing your arguments, it is helpful to look back to something to draw from and/or organize:

- For starters, **read through the assignment packet** (don't be afraid of it!) and take notes on the following: What are the facts of the case? Which side am I representing? What did the lower court decide? Where (i.e., in what jurisdiction) was the trial heard/decision made? Who is appealing the lower court decision? Where is the appeal being heard? What issue(s) is/are being appealed?

- **Get your feet wet in some legal research.**
    - Background research: Spend 2-3 hours doing some background research. Specifically, read secondary sources about the issue(s) that are being appealed. (Please refer to Chapter 9 for specific tips on finding secondary sources.) Read to find out basic information about the legal issue. Take notes on the following: What is the law, or what is the rule? Do different jurisdictions handle the law differently (i.e., are there different rules based on what state you're in)?

2) Research case precedent.

Once you have completed the background research, find out how courts have handled the issue, or a similar legal issue, in the past. Put frankly, here are the questions you are seeking to answer while conducting research:

- The court in which the appeal is being brought
  - Fact-based precedent: Has this court decided another case that has the same, or similar, facts as my case? If so, read those case opinions. Jot down the citations.
  - Legal-issue based precedent: Has this court decided another case that has the same, or similar, legal issues as my case? If so, read those case opinions. Jot down the citations.

- Higher courts (i.e. "binding authority")
  - Fact-based precedent: Has a higher court decided a case with the same, or similar, facts as my case?
  - Legal-issue based precedent: Has a higher court decided a case with the same, or similar, legal issue that is being contested in my case?

- Horizontal courts (i.e. "persuasive authority")
  - Fact-based precedent: Have courts in other jurisdictions decided on a similar set of facts?
  - Legal-issue based precedent: Have courts in other jurisdictions decided on this particular legal issue, or a similar issue?

Regarding binding authority vs. persuasive authority: Binding authority (sometimes referred to as "mandatory authority") is a case, statute, or regulation that the court must follow; it is a source of law that binds the court. In other words, the decision from a higher court is *binding* to lower courts. On the other hand, persuasive authority is a case or secondary source that can persuade the court, but has no legal power to bind the court to a particular outcome, and the court does not have to consider it in reaching its conclusion. Common sources of persuasive authority are decisions from a lower court, decisions from a horizontal court, and secondary sources like legal encyclopedias, treatises, law reviews, and research studies.

Example: Binding vs. Persuasive Authority in the Federal Court System
(Refer to diagram below to follow the example explained below.)

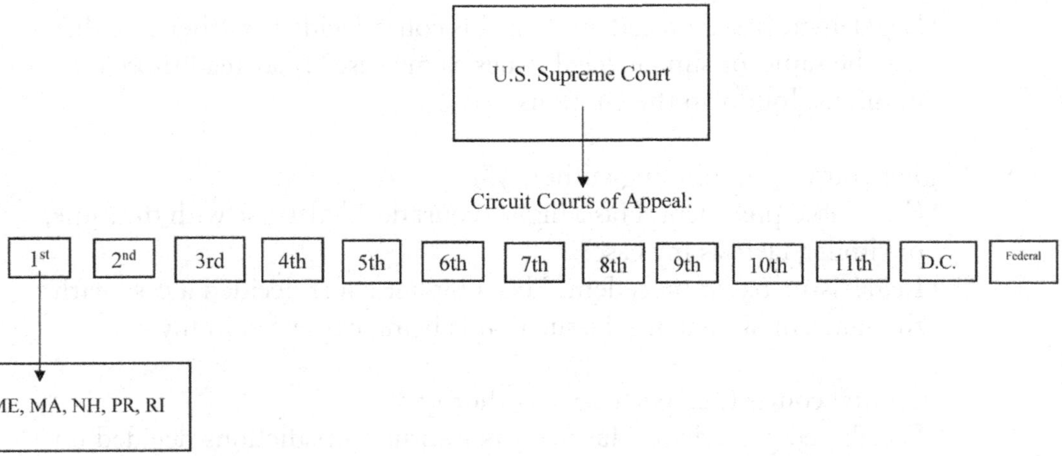

In regards to the federal court system, decisions from the Supreme Court are binding to the 13 Circuit Courts of Appeal. Also, a decision from the First Circuit Court of Appeals is binding to the federal district courts in Maine, Massachusetts, New Hampshire, Puerto Rico, and Rhode Island. However, a decision from the Fifth Circuit Court of Appeals does not bind the First Circuit Court of Appeals (or any of the courts within the 1st Circuit). A decision from the Fifth Circuit Court of Appeals can, however, be used to **persuade** the First Circuit Court of Appeals (or any of the district courts within the 1st Circuit) to rule similarly about an issue.

Obviously, you want to use as much binding authority as possible to support your arguments. However, do not throw out case law from another jurisdiction just because it is not binding. You may be able to use it to persuade the court to act like a horizontal court. Examples of how to introduce persuasive authority:

"For instance, the First Circuit's approach is to ..." OR

"We may look to the First Circuit for persuasive authority. In *John Doe v. Jane Doe* … [then go on to explain the case, the outcome, legal reasoning, etc. and how it could be adopted to the case at hand.] OR

"According to the Second Restatement of Torts … [then go on to explain what the secondary source states and tie it into your argument.]"

- Also, be sure to take note of the cases that work for your client, as well as those that do not. Obviously, you want to save the cases that work because you may be able to use them in your argument. You also want to save unfavorable cases (if they are binding authority) because you have an ethical responsibility not to knowingly omit any binding authority that is not in your client's favor. One way to handle unfavorable cases that are binding law is to differentiate your case from unfavorable case precedent. Present argument(s) to persuade the court to treat your case differently: Does your case introduce something (i.e., facts, a line of reasoning) that was not considered in the original case precedent? Or, conversely, does your case *lack* something that the original case precedent has? Has there been some significant change (for instance, in society or the legal field) since the original case precedent? Get creative in how you differentiate your case from a binding case that is not in your client's favor.

- Lastly, be sure to keep track of which court said what, and jot down the case citations. You will be thankful that your research is organized when you begin to write your brief.

3) Brainstorm arguments.

Based on your research, brainstorm all possible arguments you want to present in your brief by writing down the point(s) you want to prove. Brainstorming the point(s) you want to prove will help to winnow down your thoughts to the strongest argument for your brief.

Use what you have learned from reading the secondary sources and the case law precedent to "back up" why you think the case should come out a certain way. It may be necessary to go back and find more case precedent while brainstorming arguments.

- If you get frustrated, just take a minute to walk away, go for a run, cook, head to the coffee shop for your favorite dessert, and come back re-charged. Just remember, this is a process. I remember spending at least a week or two on simply crafting the arguments (and searching for supporting case precedent). I also remember having to throw out some arguments. Again, it is a process; be patient with yourself.

- Law firms and legal organizations have collaborative business meetings to figure out what arguments to present, so have fun with this step! Typically, at some point in time during the argument creation phase, you should meet with your team to present the ideas you have come up with. By the end of the brainstorming session(s), you and your teammates should have decided on the top (i.e., two to four) best arguments.

- While most of your argument should be based on the law and legal reasoning, one or more of your arguments may be policy arguments. Policy arguments state what the law *should* be to achieve some good, societal benefit. Depending on the preferences of your instructor, policy arguments may/may not have been welcome in your legal memo; however, they are common in briefs. Whereas the legal arguments in your brief will be based on case precedent, policy arguments may be based on psychology, statistics, history, science, human behavior, economics, and a plethora of other fields. Whatever you choose to base your policy argument on, just make sure your reasoning is logical and explained with clarity. It is also helpful and impressive if your policy arguments cite to non-legal authority such as a reputable journal, report, research study, etc. Verify with your instructor (or supervising attorney) whether policy arguments are permitted and/or expected in your brief assignment. If so, then use this moment to move away from the traditional CRuPAC formula to explain why, based on good, sound societal policy, the court should rule a certain way.

4) Decide on a theory of the case.

The theory of the case explains why your client should win. It is the narrative that you will weave throughout the brief that ties together the facts, case precedent, and policy considerations to persuade the court to rule a certain way. In one to two sentences, the theory of the case answers the question, "What is this case about?" It is not an explicit part of the brief with its own section; instead, the theory of the case is something you formulate before you begin writing your brief to help frame your arguments. Think of it as the overall theme for your brief. Here are some guiding steps to help you form a theory of the case:

- Based on the facts of the case, the background legal research, and the case precedent research, brainstorm the theory of the case with your partners. Typically, a brief is written in a team, so you and your partner(s) should discuss the narrative you will use to persuade the court to rule in your client's favor. By the end of the brainstorming session, you should have decided on a theory of the case.

- Remember, the purpose of the brief is to persuade, so be sure to frame your theory in a way that is favorable to your client.

- In terms of brief writing, the theory of the case should name the relevant legal principles.

- In terms of brief writing, the theory of the case should also include the strongest policy argument.

EXAMPLE

This case is about a law school infringing on the due process rights of law students by suddenly mandating uniforms when uniform attire had never been required, is not required by any other law school, and deprives students of their individuality.

> This theory of the case frames the issue by naming the legal principal of "due process."

5) Outline your arguments. (i.e., Create a working outline of your brief.)

Now that you have conducted some background research, chosen your best arguments, and decided on a theory of the case, (and probably went back to conduct more research in-between), it is now time to put it all together. Create an outline that clearly lists your arguments. As you list each argument, also include the citation to the case precedent on which the argument is based.

Now is also a good time to order your arguments. There are varying opinions on how the arguments in a legal brief should be ordered. Ultimately the choice is yours, but here are some suggestions:

- Begin with a dispositive argument. That is, begin with the argument that would resolve the issue on its own, without the help of the other arguments.

- Begin with your strongest argument.

- Begin with the argument that easy to understand, then introduce the argument that requires complex legal or technical reasoning.

- Embed "weak" argument in-between the stronger arguments.

- Make sure legal arguments come before policy arguments.

- Save new, innovative reasoning for last. Begin with legal arguments and maneuvers that will be familiar to the court.

- Do not begin with an argument/subject the court does not like to rule on. Specifically, appellate courts typically do not like to decide issues about the Constitution, so some attorneys save their constitutional arguments for last.

6) Fully form your arguments.

For legal-based analyses, flush out your arguments by outlining CRuPACs.

For policy-based reasoning, flush out your arguments by clearly explaining what the law should be, or how the court should rule, and why. Again, the "why" may be based on journals, books, studies, or reports from various non-legal fields.

Writing your Brief

◇◇◇◇◇◇◇

Structure

The basic components of a legal brief are as follows:

I. Cover Page

II. Table of Contents

III. Table of Authorities

IV. Preliminary Statement

V. Question(s) Presented

VI. Statement of Facts

VII. Summary of Argument

VIII. Argument

IX. Conclusion

X. Signature Block

Please refer to your instructor's guidelines regarding specifics for format and content for your brief. Also, appellate courts typically have a specified format that legal briefs must follow, so be sure to refer to the court or jurisdictional guidelines. However, here are generic guidelines, tips, and examples for a basic brief.

I. Cover Page

Definitely refer to your instructor's (or the court's) guidelines for the content and format of the cover page. Generally speaking, however, the cover page should include:

- The court in which the appeal is being heard (i.e., "In the Supreme Court of the State of Nevada")
- Case number

- Case caption clearly denoting the plaintiff, the defendant, the appellant, and the appellee. The appellant is the party who requested the appeal. The appellee is the party who is responding to the appeal. In the following example, the appellant is the plaintiff, and the defendant is the appellee. Refer to your assignment to make sure you correctly note who is the appellant and appellee.

EXAMPLE

OLIVER BROWN, et. al
PLAINTIFFS-APPELLANT
V.
BOARD OF EDUCATION OF TOPEKA, KANSAS, et al.
DEFENDANT-APPELLEE

Brief of Appellant

Attorney 1 Name
Bar Number
Attorney 2 Name
Bar Number
Attorneys for Plaintiffs-Appellant

II. Table of Contents

Include page numbers for the main components of your brief. Again, this will differ according to what your instructor, or the court, requires.

- Table of Authorities
- Preliminary Statement
- Questions Presented
- Statement of Facts
- Summary of Argument
- Argument

Note: Within the argument section of the table of contents, also include the page numbers for point headings and subheadings/subtitles. (The point headings are the major points of your argument, and subheadings/subtitles are the minor points that support the major points.)

Point Heading #1

Subheading

Point Heading #2

Subheading

Point Heading #3

Subheading

- Conclusion

III. Table of Authorities

A table of authorities is a list of all the cases, statutes, restatements, and even research articles you mention in the brief. List the authorities in categories (i.e. "Cases," "Statutes," "Restatements," "Other Authorities"). Within each category, alphabetize the list.

IV. Preliminary Statement

A preliminary statement may/may not be required; be sure to check your professor's and/or the court's expectations. In five to eight sentences, it briefly explains the appeal to someone who has no idea about the case, so it includes:

- A brief explanation of how the case arose. (What action initiated the suit?)

- The procedural posture. That is, what is the legal, procedural history of the case?
  - What court's decision is being appealed?
  - Is the decision from a trial or other type of hearing? If it was a trial, was it before a judge or jury?
  - What was the determination of the case by the court below?
  - On what grounds is the appellant appealing?

EXAMPLE

Notice how I am already framing the case by using certain adverbs to describe the facts. This is an example of weaving the theory of the case into the brief.

In the Fall of 2017, The University of No-State Law School suddenly imposed mandatory uniforms on the entire student body, including candidates for the Juris Doctor (J.D.), the Master of Laws (LL.M.), and the Doctor of Juridical Science (S.J.D.). Given the abrupt mandate, student representatives from each program of study filed suit to prohibit the new policy, arguing that the mandatory uniform policy was prohibited by state law, No-State Statute §894.2, which prohibits educational institutions from putting undue burdens on students. This appeal follows a judge-issued ruling in The 14th District Trial Court of Fake Disputes, which decided that it was within the law school's power and discretion to require mandatory student uniforms and that the policy was not excessively burdensome for students. Plaintiffs appeal on the grounds that the mandatory uniform policy violates state and Constitutional law.

Again, an instance of framing the case. I am subtly preparing the court for my argument.

The decision being appealed was determined by a judge.

Decision of the lower court

Grounds of the appeal

V. Question(s) Presented

State the question(s) that you want the court to rule on. Also, note that there may be more than one legal issue/question.

- Keep the question presented short. Check with your instructor or supervisor, but as a rule of thumb, I was taught to keep the question presented to seventy-five words or less, or between one and two sentences. However, depending on the jurisdiction, complexity of the legal issue, and/or the preferred approach of the legal team, the question presented may reach three sentences.
- Formula: Include a major premise (the law or legal issue) and minor premise (key facts). Make sure there is a clear distinction between the law and the facts.
- The question presented is typically the conclusion stated as a question, or as a statement beginning with "whether." Modern briefs tend to use the first format, as opposed to beginning with "whether."
- Unless you are instructed otherwise, stay away from mentioning "appellant" or "appellee" in the question presented.
- Do not make a legal conclusion in the question presented.

EXAMPLE

Questions Presented:

Facts

1. Do the mandatory uniforms imposed by The University of No-State Law School present an "undue burden" for law students?

Law/legal issue. This will become more clear as you build your legal vocabulary, but "undue burden" is a legal term taken from the (fake) federal statute.

Law/legal issue

Facts

2. Is it a violation of Constitutional due process for The University of No-State Law School to require mandatory uniforms?

VI. Statement of Facts

Include all the factual information necessary to lay out your argument before the court. Below are some guidelines:

- Make sure the "Facts" section includes all the facts that you mention in the "Argument" section.
- Even if the assignment requires that you gather the facts from multiple sources, organize the facts in a way that is easy to understand, which typically turns out to be chronologically. In complex cases, organizing the facts thematically may make more sense. First, write a generic Facts section to get started. Then, as you complete your CRuPACs, go back and edit the Facts section as necessary, adding facts you included in your analysis (i.e. in the CRuPACs), and deleting facts that turned out to be insignificant.
- The Facts section of a legal brief should be a bit persuasive. Do not lie. Do not exaggerate. Do not omit bad facts. But keep in mind that the purpose of the brief is to persuade, and the facts should follow suit. Therefore, strategize how to incorporate bad facts. Again, do not completely omit facts that do not work in your favor. Instead, minimize the effect of bad facts by:
    - Using the passive voice instead of the active voice. Example:

      Dave assaulted the driver. (Active voice)

      The driver was assaulted by Dave. (Passive voice)

    - Mention the bad facts, but mention them quickly. Do not spend too much time on them. (My 1L instructor referred to this as not giving bad facts too much "air time.")
    - Embed a bad fact in the midst of good facts.
    - Provide a good fact immediately after the bad fact.

EXAMPLE

The University of No-State Law School is the premier law school of No-State. (R. at 1.) It is one of only two public law schools in the state. *Id.* The law school offers a Juris Doctor (J.D.) and a Master of Laws (LL.M.) program that teaches students the fundamentals of the legal profession. (R. at 11.) Most students who graduate from the J.D. or LL.M. programs go on to sit for the No-State bar. (R. at 9.) The law school also offers a Doctor of Juridical Science (S.J.D.) program for those who want to conduct advanced research in the legal field. (R. at 11.) Those who graduate from the S.J.D. program often go on to become law professors.

"R. at 1" means that the previous statement can be found on p. 1 of the record. You should be provided the record as part of the brief assignment.

Remember, Id. is a short-hand signal meaning, "The citation for what I just wrote is the immediately preceding authority." In other words, the citation for the statement, "It is one of only two public law schools in the state," is (R. at 1)

On September 21, 2017 The University of No-State Law School notified students via email that beginning the spring 2018 semester, a mandatory dress code would be instituted for all students enrolled in the school's J.D., LL.M., and S.J.D. programs. (R. at 5.) For the past three years, a document stating that the law school was considering instituting a mandatory dress code was included in the admissions packets, and newly-admitted students were required to sign the notice. *Id.* The email notified students of the following newly-mandated dress code:

Bad facts: These are bad facts for the Plaintiff-Appellant (i.e. the law school students, because it shows that they were given warning that the law school was considering mandating uniforms.) Notice how this bad fact is mentioned quickly, and embedded within the middle of the Facts section.

When attending classes on the campus of The University of No-State Law School, all law students must adhere to the following dress code. Students who refuse to comply will be immediately expelled. Per No-State Law School policy, expelled students are not allowed to attend classes, be on the school's property, or register for classes. However, if a student does not wish to comply with the mandatory dress code policy, she is permitted to enroll in the online division of the school. Although individuals who complete the law school's online program are able to take an online version of all on-campus classes, online students do not receive a law degree. Instead, they receive a Certificate of Continuing Education. Also, online students are not permitted to attend office hours unless they arrive with the appropriate, mandated attire, as office hours are conducted on-campus.

- All women must wear dress slacks or skirts that are no higher than one-inch above the knee. The permitted color for women's bottoms are black, navy blue, and dark brown.

- Men must wear dress slacks at all time. The permitted color for men's bottoms are black, navy blue, and dark brown.

- Regardless of gender, blouses may not contain any writing. Permitted designs for blouses are: polka-dot, stripes, and no design. There is no restriction on the color of blouses.

- Regardless of gender, all students must wear suit jackets to class, in the library, or when representing the law school at an off-campus event. Once students arrive to class or the library, they are permitted to remove their suit jacket.

- Regardless of gender, all students must wear dress shoes to class. Women are not required to wear high-heels. However, flats must be office-appropriate. Tennis shoes, sneakers, running shoes, flip-flops, and sandals are not permitted. (R. at 16.)

Two weeks after the law school sent the email notifying students of the new dress code, it published a manual. (R. at 15.) The manual provided the law school's rationale for instituting the mandatory uniform policy, "The purpose of this policy is to prepare students for the real-world expectations of working in the legal field. Clients, judges, the government, and the general public look to the legal profession to uphold the law, defend, prosecute, and achieve justice. We must make our students aware of such responsibility and the importance of looking the part. Furthermore, most law firms, public-interest organizations, and courts follow a similar dress code. As an institution of legal education, we have the responsibility to prepare our students for what is to come. (R. at 24.)

On January 25, 2018, the first day of the spring 2018 semester, three students – Ode Zariq, a J.D. candidate; David Whimsey, an LL.M. candidate; and Nat Battles, an S.J.D. candidate, each attended their respective classes in violation of the dress code. (R. at 34.) Ode Zariq wore a t-shirt with the word "REBEL" written across the front, blue jean pants, and tennis shoes. (R. at 36.) David Whimsey wore a striped shirt with khaki shorts. *Id.* Nat Battles wore a casual t-shirt with loose-fitting cargo pants. *Id.* On January 26, 2018 all three students received hand-delivered notices that they had been expelled from school. *Id.* When they tried to attend class, they were escorted off the premises, kicking and screaming. (R. at 40.)

VII. Summary of Argument

The purpose of the Summary of Argument is to clue the reader in on the arguments that will be presented in the brief; it acts as a roadmap.

- It may be helpful to first complete the argument section before completing the Summary of Argument. I suggest skipping ahead, now, to the explanation and example of the Argument section, as the Summary of the Argument will make more sense after you have read the full Argument (and understand all of the pieces of the Argument).
- Approach the Summary of Argument by expanding the point headings into a few sentences (or one paragraph, at most). Expand the point headings by applying the most compelling facts of the case to the rule(s).
- Identify the standard of review. Example:

Example

The dress code policy of the University of No-State Law School is an undue burden for law students because it restricts law students from obtaining a legal education, and such a policy is not necessary for students to receive legal training. Also, the policy violates the constitutional guarantee of due process, as it strips students of the freedom to attend class at a public institution without adequate notice or an opportunity to be heard.

> Provide a roadmap of the argument. This first paragraph is simply a restatement of all the point headings using different language.

After a bench trial Judge Camila Alvarez found that the law school's policy did not present an excessive or undue burden for law students and that it did not violate constitutional due process. This Court should reverse that decision. This court reviews a lower court's finding de novo. *Wood v. Safeway, Inc.*, 121 P.3d 1026, 1029 (Nev. 2009). Facts established as true by the lower court are accepted by this court. *Id.* Regarding constitutional issues, this court applies strict scrutiny to constitutional issues that bear on fundamental or due process rights. *Wrinkle v. State Department of Housing*, 23 P.3d 34, 90 (2015). The statute, or policy, must be "narrowly tailored" to address a "compelling state interest." *Id.*

> Before I identify the standard of review I give a brief background of what has happened thus far in the case and what action I would like the court to take.

> Explain the standard of review.

The mandatory dress code presents an undue burden for students enrolled in The University of No-State Law School.

> Address each argument, one by one, by completing an abbreviated CRuPAC.
> 1) State the conclusion
> 2) State the rule(s).
> 3) BRIEFLY apply the most compelling facts to the rule.
> This paragraph addresses the first argument that will be presented in the Argument section (labeled by **Roman numeral I** in the Argument section).

No-State Statute §894.2 prohibits educational institutions from putting undue burdens on students. A school policy is unduly burdensome if non-compliance with the policy restricts student learning and its implementation is not necessary for students to learn. *Univ. of Fake v. Robins*, 255 P.3d 238, 246, *Lee v. Made-up University*, P.3d 209, 212 (Nevada 2016). The mandatory uniform policy of The University of No-State Law School restricts learning because students who do not adhere to the dress code are not permitted to register for on-campus classes, attend on-campus classes, or visit professors during offi ce hours. Also, the mandatory uniforms are not a necessary requirement for student learning, since law students are able to learn the law and perform clinical work without clothing items such as suit jackets and dress shoes.

Also, the mandatory uniform policy is not narrowly tailored to meet a compelling state interest. When the court is considering whether a policy or statute violates a fundamental or due process right, the strict scrutiny test is applied. *Wrinkle v. State Department of Housing*, 23 P.3d 34, 90 (2015). To pass strict scrutiny, the policy must satisfy three tests: 1) It must be justified by a compelling governmental interest; 2) The policy must be narrowly tailored to achieve that goal or interest; and 3) The law or policy must be the least restrictive means for achieving that goal or interest. *Id.* The law school's manual states that the purpose of the policy is to "prepare

This paragraph addresses the second argument that will be presented in the Argument section (labeled by **Roman numeral II** in the Argument section).

students for the real-world expectations of working in the legal field," and to stress the "importance of looking the part." (R. at 24.) However, preparing students for real-world expectations and "looking the part" of the legal field are not compelling government interests. Also, the uniform policy is not narrowly tailored to such a goal because it infringes on the liberty of law students who, for instance, will not be entering traditional legal careers that require a professional style of dress. Finally, requiring students to work under an attorney or train under a judge are least restrictive means to achieve the law school's goal of preparation for the legal field.

This paragraph addresses the third argument that will be presented in the Argument section (labeled by **Roman numeral III** in the Argument section).

Also, the dress code policy of The University of No-State Law School is a violation of due process guaranteed in the Fifth and Fourteenth Amendments of the U.S. Constitution. *See* U. S. Const. amend. IV and XIV. Procedural due process requires the government, or state actors, to follow procedures before taking away an individual's life, liberty, or property. *Blah v. Blah Government*, 34 Blah Blah Journal 34 (2000). Specifically, the government must provide the individual with notice, an opportunity to be heard, and a decision by a neutral decision maker. *Id.* As a public state university The University of No-State Law School is a state actor. However, the uniform policy enacted by the university does not fulfill all the procedural requirements that are necessary before the law school can deny students their liberty. Although noncompliant students are provided with a notice, they are then immediately expelled with no opportunity to be heard before a tribunal, judge, mediator, or other neutral decision maker. Where the mandatory uniform policy is an undue burden for students, where the uniform policy is not narrowly tailored to a compelling state interest, and where it violates constitutional due process, policy dictates that the mandatory uniform policy of The University of No-State Law School be declared an undue burden and unconstitutional.

VIII. Argument

The argument is the "meat" of your brief. Most of your arguments will be legal, and some may be policy-based. For legal arguments, use the CRuPAC formula. Make sure to organize the argument section by using point headings and subheadings/subtitles.

Point Headings – Use point headings for the main arguments of your brief. Typically, point headings consist of two parts:

1. A conclusion that you want the court to accept OR an action you want the court to take, and

> Example: "The court should grant the motion to suppress."

2. The reason why the court should accept the conclusion (or take the proffered action).
   - Introduce the second part by using, "because."

Subheadings (aka, Subtitles) – use subheadings as necessary to support the main, point headings. Note, subheadings are not always necessary; use them when there are multiple elements in the point heading that need to be addressed (i.e., CRuPAC'ed) individually.

> The following is an introductory paragraph, introducing the first argument of the brief. Before you "dig in" to complete the legal analysis of each the argument, take a moment to do a quick introduction of each argument by CruPAC'ing the main point heading. For starters, the first "C" (of the introductory CRuPAC) is the point heading, itself, so start the paragraph with the Rule statement.

EXAMPLE

I. The uniforms imposed by the University of No-State Law School are an undue burden for students because they severely restrict learning and are not necessary for legal training.

A school policy restricts learning if non-compliance with the policy results in student expulsion or suspension, significant absences, or disengagement with course content or professors. *Univ. of Fake v. Robins,* 255 P.3d 238, 246, *Lee v. Made-up University,* P.3d 209, 212 (Nevada 2016). The mandatory uniform policy of the University of No-State Law School restricts learning because students who do not comply are not permitted to attend school. Also, a school policy is deemed unnecessary if omission of the policy does not hinder, or otherwise negatively affect, student learning. *Sanchez v. Anonymous Medical School,* 221 P.3d 246, 252 (Nevada 2017). Mandatory school uniforms are unnecessary because not dressing in lawyer and/or business attire does not hinder, or otherwise negatively affect, students from learning the law and/or receiving legal training.

First Point Heading: This is the first argument of the brief. Notice the construction of the point heading:
1) The conclusion I want the court to accept: The uniforms imposed by the University of No-State Law School are an undue burden for students.
2) The reason the court should accept the conclusion: … because they severely restrict learning and are not necessary for legal training.
Also notice that for this first point heading, there are two elements that need to be proven/argued to show that the uniforms are an undue burden: that the uniforms "severely restrict learning" and are "not necessary for legal training." Hence, this point heading will have two subheadings.

Rule #1: This will become subheading #1 of your first point heading/argument

Proof #1

Application-Conclusion #1

Rule #2: This will become subheading #2 of your first point heading/argument

Proof #2

Application-Conclusion #2

1) Mandatory uniforms severely restrict students of The University of No-State Law School from learning.

A school policy severely restricts learning if non-compliance with the policy results in student expulsion or suspension, significant absences, or disengagement with the course content or professors. *Univ. of Fake v. Robins,* 255 P.3d 238, 246, *Lee v. Made-up University,* P.3d 209, 212 (Nevada 2016). In the case at hand, "all law students must adhere to the dress code," and students who do not are immediately expelled. (R at 16.) Hence, non-complying students would not be able to engage with the course content or professors because upon expulsion they would be barred from enrolling in class, attending class, and being present on campus. Although students in violation of the dress code are permitted to attend the online division of the law school, the online option results in disengagement with the course professors, since noncompliant, online students are unable to attend office hours.

Furthermore, noncompliant students are unlikely to enroll in the online division because completing the online program does not result in a J.D., LL.M., or S.J.D., credentials that act as verification that a law student has received adequate legal training. Hence, the on-campus program is the only, viable option for law students to learn the law in a program that equips them with the academic credentials necessary to move

Subheading #1: CRuPAC the first legal issue of your first argument. The first "C" of this CRuPAC is the subheading, itself, so begin the paragraph with the Rule statement.

Rule for subheading #1

Proof for subheading #1

Application/Analysis for subheading #1. This analysis is based on applying the rule statement to the facts of the case at hand. Rule statement: "A school policy severely restricts learning if non-compliance with the policy results in student expulsion or suspension, significant abscences, or disengagement wit the course content o professors." Facts of the case at hand: Students who don't comply with th dresscode policy are barred from enrolling class, attending class, and being present on camp Also, if you prefer, you can also do an analys where you are comparing (or contrasting) the ca precedent with the ca at hand. I did not do s here, but that is definitely another analytical strategy.

If applicable, address the argument the other side is likely to bring up.

forward in their legal careers. The mandatory uniform policy of The University of No-State Law School severely restricts students from receiving a legal education.

> **Conclusion for subheading #1**

2) In order to receive adequate legal education and training, it is not necessary for law students to wear prescribed, mandated attire.

> **Subheading #2:** CRuPAC the second legal issue of your first argument. The first "C" of this CRuPAC is the subheading, itself, so begin the paragraph with the Rule statement.

A school policy is deemed unnecessary if omission of the policy does not hinder, or otherwise negatively affect, student learning. *Sanchez v. Anonymous Medical School,* 221 P.3d 246, 252 (Nevada 2017). In *Sanchez,* Anonymous Medical School instituted a policy requiring all candidates for the Medical Doctor degree (M.D.) to wear medical scrubs, a white lab coat, and a stethoscope during clinical courses, residency, and whenever they engaged in training at a medical facility or clinic. *Id.* at 253. Sanchez sued the school on the grounds that the mandatory uniform policy presented an undue burden on learning. *Id.* The court disagreed and held that the dress code requirements did not hinder medical students from learning. In fact, the court found that the uniform helped the students in three, distinct ways. First, it mimicked the functional attire the students would wear as physicians. Second, it allowed other medical staff and personnel to identify the students. And third, the stethoscope was a helpful learning tool, as it

> **Rule for subheading #2**

> **Proof for subheading #2**

> **Application/ Analysis:** This begins the application/analysis for subheading #2

> When explaining complex precedent, don't be afraid to use transition words that help the reader follow the line of logic.

allowed the students to practice how they would use the stethoscopes in real-life situations with patients. *Id.*

This paragraph is still a continuation of the Application/ Analysis of subheading #2. It argues that the court should come out differently from the case precedent by contrasting the case precedent against the case at hand, and arguing why, based on those different facts, this court should come out differently.

Unlike the uniform policy in *Sanchez*, which required its students to adhere to the prescribed dress code when engaged in training in a medical facility, or during clinicals and residency, The University of No-State Law School requires its students to wear uniforms whenever they are attending an on-campus class. Also, the Anonymous Medical School policy is based on practical considerations such as personnel in a medical facility being able to recognize students as medically-trained individuals in case, for instance, a patient needs medical assistance. However, the uniform policy mandated by the University of No-State Law School is not based on such practical considerations. After all, there is no need, for instance, for a lawyer, paralegal, or client to be able to identify a law student as legally-trained while the law student is sitting in the classroom or elsewhere on campus. Finally, the Anonymous Medical School policy that requires students to wear stethoscopes is beneficial to student learning because it allows the medical students to train using a real medical device that they will likely use once they are certified physicians. On the other hand, suit jackets, dress bottoms, and dress shoes do not help a law student prepare for the real-world of drafting legal memos, understanding complex statutes, or explaining difficult law to clients. The uniform policy of The University of No-State Law School is not necessary for its students to receive a legal education.

Conclusion of subheading #2

I did not include examples of a full, written legal analysis for Point Heading II and Point Heading III. Instead, I present a reminder of how to structure the arguments (Point Headings + subheadings + CRuPACs) for your brief:

II. The dress code policy is not narrowly tailored to address a compelling state interest.

> **Second Point Heading:** This is the second argument of your brief.
> In this example, according to the case law there are three elements that need to be proven/ argued about the uniform policy:
> *whether it is narrowly tailored
> *whether it is justified by a compelling state interest
> *whether it is the least restrictive means
> Hence, this point heading/ argument will have three subheadings.

[Insert introductory CRuPAC for this point heading. That is, write a paragraph that is an overarching, generalized CRuPAC that generally applies the facts to the point heading.]

1) The uniform policy is not narrowly tailored.

> **Subheading #1:** CRuPAC the first legal issue of this argument. The first "C" of the subheading's CRuPAC is the subheading, itself, so begin the paragraph with the Rule statement.

[Insert CRuPAC analysis that defines/explains "narrowly tailored."]

2) The law school's uniform policy is not justified by a compelling state interest.

[Insert CRuPAC analysis that defines "justified by a compelling governmental interest."]

3) The law school's uniform policy is not the least restrictive means for achieving the goal of preparing students to enter the legal profession.

> **Subheading #3:** CRuPAC the third legal issue of this argument. The first "C" of the subheading's CRuPAC is the subheading, itself, so begin the paragraph with the Rule statement.

[Insert CRuPAC analysis that explains/defines "least restrictive means."]

III. It is a violation of procedural due process for the University of No-State Law School to require mandatory uniforms because the students were not given an opportunity to be heard.

> **Third Point Heading:** This is the third argument of the brief.
> Notice that I did not include an introductory CRuPAC after this point heading. I chose not to do so because the analysis for this point heading is very short – I'm only analyzing one legal issue, "opportunity to be heard."

EXAMPLE

[Insert CRuPAC analysis of cases that define "opportunity to be heard,"]

Although it is ideal if you can find cases that are specifically about **students'** opportunity to be heard, that is not necessary. You can use cases from legal topics that are non-related to students, universities, or schools, so long as they define "opportunity to be heard."

IV. Mandatory uniforms will negatively affect the emotional and psychological well-being of law students.

Fourth Point Heading: This is the fourth argument of the brief.
The following is an example of a policy argument. It isn't focused on what the law is, but what the law should be. Use evidence, books, reports, etc. from another field – economics, political science, statistics, or in this case (fake) psychology – to persuade the court. Notice how the policy argument is introduced last, after the legal analyses.

A recent study published in *Fictional Psychology Journal* found that "requiring individuals above the age of 21 to dress uniformly significantly decreases their happiness." Jim Carey, *The Effect of Uniforms on Adults,* 320 Fictional Psychology J.72 (2016). The article wherein the study was published went on to explain that because uniforms decrease an individual's opportunity to engage in self-expression and individuality, the individual feels less free to be herself. As a result of this loss of freedom, personal happiness declines. One can certainly see how this applies in the context of law school. Law schools attract students from diverse backgrounds. Take, for instance, an incoming first-year law student (1L) class. It is bound to have a plethora of races, ethnicities, and cultures represented. Moreover, diverse ways of life are sure to exist within each 1L class: the mid-career professional who has become accustomed to professional dress; the young student who just wrapped up her undergraduate education and doesn't mind wearing leggings, an oversized t-shirt, and a baseball cap to class; the hipster tech genius who has spent the last couple of years wearing jeans and a t-shirt to his technology

Unless instructed otherwise, you may structure your policy argument however you want. Do whatever you (and your team) think will be most persuasive. Here, I used the Quote and Comment method (explained in Chapter 1 and Chapter 12).
Also, this is just one policy argument. You may have more, if space permits.

EXAMPLE

firm; and the list goes on and on. 90% of Americans agree with the statement that "style of dress is an integral part of my identity." James Williams, *Dress Codes and Identity*, 320 Fake Anthropology Journal 72, 89 (2017). Although law students have converged in one place, i.e., the law school, to obtain a legal education, they are still individuals with unique identities that are worth expressing. It would do the law school, and society, a disservice to ask these unique individuals to mask a part of their identity. After all, law students are those who will make the law, defend the law, and change the law. It is not in the best interest of society for the creators, defenders, and upholders of the law to be a robotic, uniform body that conforms to one look. Instead, it is best for lawyers to be able to relate to various sectors of society and diverse groups of Americans. Hence, before they become lawyers, law students should be able to obtain their legal education while experiencing the happiness that results from the individual self-expression of choosing their own attire.

IX. Conclusion

Do not summarize your argument. Restate the relief sought (i.e. how you would like the court to rule) and the grounds on which your request should be granted. Example:

> For these reasons, the Association of Law Students requests that the court reverse the judgment.

X. Signature Block

The attorneys sign the brief. The signature block should appear after the last sentence of the conclusion and be aligned to the right side of the document.

EXAMPLE

CONCLUSION

For these reasons, the Association of Law Students requests that the court reverse the judgment.

Respectfully submitted,

[insert signature]

Jane Doe, *Esq.*

[insert signature]

John Doe, *Esq.*

Attorneys for Plaintiff-Appellant

CHAPTER 12

LEGAL RESEARCH PAPERS

Sometimes in law school your midterm or final will not be an Issue-Spotter exam, legal memo, or brief, but you will have to write a research paper about some aspect of the law or some legally-related topic. For those instances in law school when I was given free rein to write a research paper without adhering to an imposed legal structure, I would approach the writing assignment in the same way I approached my college writing assignments as an undergraduate. The only difference was that as a law student, my sources, commentary, and observation(s) were, in some facet, related to the law.

SOURCES

Legal Sources

When writing a research paper in law school, the sources you will use to conduct your research will typically be either a ***legal*** source or a ***non-legal*** source.

- The actual text of laws, regulations, or cases (These are primary sources. They are also called "authorities" in the legal profession.)

- A document that is the product of the legal system, or a product of the process of law making (Examples: the transcript of a trial or jury deliberations; a report issued by the U.S. Department of Justice; the legislative history of a certain law.)

- Articles from law reviews and legal journals, books, interviews, etc. that comment on or provide insight about the law or some part of the legal process.

Non-Legal Sources

Alternatively, depending on the topic and purpose of your paper, you may find that you use ***non-legal*** sources. This happens when you are writing a paper about a legal topic, but other fields of study offer pertinent insight to help you answer your research question or learn more about the law, its causes, effects, etc. For instance, in a criminal theory course I wrote a final paper about the use of fingerprint evidence in criminal trials. Although I cited to articles from law reviews and legal journals, a hefty amount of my paper was based on sources from the fields of statistics, forensic science, and psychology. Non-legal sources for legal research papers are limitless, but may include:

- Articles, books, and professional journals from various disciplines
- Interviews, documentaries, newspaper articles, etc.
- Historical texts
- Surveys
- A plethora of other sources of information

The Quote and Comment Approach, Law School

◇◇◇◇◇◇◇

Use the Quote and Comment approach when you want to: 1) answer a particular research question, or 2) learn about a particular subject. As you complete the research and draft your writing plan, the answer(s) to your research question will become clear.

The Quote and Comment Formula

1) Gather your sources.

- A primary authority is the actual law. Examples:

  - a law, statute, regulation, constitution, or case, OR
  - documents that are the product of the legal system or the legal process (i.e. trial transcript, legislative history, resolutions from the UN, the text of a contract, etc.)
- A secondary source is a writing about the law. A secondary source summarizes, explains, or provides commentary or insight about a certain law, the legal process, or legal actor. Examples:
  - treatises, hornbooks, restatements of the law, model penal codes, books, articles interviews, documentaries, etc.

2) Read.

Now it is time to go digging through all of those sources to find the information you need. Do not be intimated by the thickness of the books or the length of articles. After all, you are not reading these sources leisurely, like you would read a fictional novel or a comic book, but instead, you are a reader on a mission. **You are reading to pull out specific information for your paper.** So, when you pick up a book, glance at the chapter titles. Hop to the chapter that you think is most pertinent to your paper. Then as you read the chapter, use your eyes as laser radars on a special assignment to detect information that you can take back to your research paper and comment on. The same goes for reading journal articles or any other source: you are reading with focus, as you are on a mission to find information to later comment on in your paper.

3) Highlight the information that stands out to you.

As you read, pull out those quotes, paragraphs, and research findings that you found interesting, or that are otherwise pertinent to your research paper. Practically speaking, this step should be a list of quotes, paragraphs, and research findings that you type (or write) verbatim from the source, into a Microsoft Word document (or onto paper). Be sure to label each quote, paragraph, or research finding with the source and page number, that way, citations are a breeze.

4) Comment on the information you highlighted.

This is where the analytical writing begins. Your commentary will be about the quote, fact, or finding found from the above sources.

Here are some ideas:

* Your opinion about the fact (or quote) you found.
* How one quote (or research finding) reminds you of something else.

* Was a research finding surprising to you?
* Compare two different quotes you found.
* Contrast two different pieces of information, or opinions you found.
* Explain how your opinion changed based on something you read.
* The ideas are limitless. Respond, in your own way, to the information you have gathered.

5) Create a plan/working outline.

Before you begin to write, you must plan! Planning gives form, structure, and purpose to your paper, making it a well-written, quality product, as opposed to random rambling just to meet a word count. Trust me, professors can tell the difference, and they are more likely to appreciate (and therefore assign a better grade to) a well-written, thought-out final product than some random sentences and ideas mindlessly pieced together.

The Quote and Comment Structure

The plan for a Quote and Comment paper is simply a list of all the research you highlighted as interesting (i.e. quotes, facts, research findings, etc. from Step 3), embedded with how you want to respond to each piece of information:

I. Quote, Fact, or Research Finding #1 (also write the citation)
 * Commentary

II. Quote, Fact, or Research Finding #2 (also write the citation)
 * Commentary

III. Quote, Fact, or Research Finding #3 (also write the citation)
 * Commentary

Add as many quotes, facts, or findings (Roman numerals) as necessary to meet the minimum word count or page limit. Also, add as many commentaries (*asterisks) as you would like under each quote, fact, or finding. Once your plan/working outline is completed, you are ready to begin writing your research paper. **Example plan/working outline of a Quote and Comment legal research paper:**

THE USE OF FINGERPRINTS IN CRIMINAL TRIALS

◇◇◇◇◇◇◇◇

I. "Although the accuracy and necessity of DNA analysis in criminal trials is long-established, recent studies and anecdotes have emerged that fingerprint analysis is not as reliable as the public assumes." Hampton B. Reich, *Reliability of Fingerprint.* 34 Fake Law Review 73, 79 (2011).

[*Insert commentary*]

[*Insert commentary*]

II. In *Daubert v. Merrell Dow Pharmaceuticals* the Supreme Court rejected precedent that stated the science underlying an expert testimony must be generally accepted by the scientific community. *See Daubert v. Merrell Dow Pharmaceuticals*, 509 US 579, 597 (1993).

Notice here that I am not commenting on a **quote**, but a **fact**. The Quote and Comment method can be used to comment on quotes, facts, research findings from scientific studies, dicta* in cases, etc. (*Dicta is everything the judge talks about in the case that is NOT the holding.)

[*Insert commentary*]

[*Insert commentary*]

III. " Of the prints that did not actually match, the experts incorrectly declared 0.68% of them as matching (false alarms)... the corresponding false alarm rate for novices was 55.18%." Matthew B. Thompson, et al., *Expertise in Fingerprint Identification,* 58 J. Forensic Sci. 1519, 1521 (2013).

Notice that this source is non-legal. Sometimes it makes sense to turn to non-legal fields to conduct research for your topic.

[*Insert commentary*]

[*Insert commentary*]

The Observe and Cite Approach, Law School

◇◇◇◇◇◇◇◇

This formula comes in handy when you already have an opinion, idea, or point you want to prove, and you want your research paper to help you prove that point.

The Observe and Cite Formula

1) Brainstorm your observation.

Write down the point you want to prove, as well as different variations of it. Brainstorming the point(s) you want to prove will help to narrow down your paper topic (and therefore make your research much easier).

In the context of law school or a legal research paper, your observation(s) will concern some aspect of the law, such as:

- The effect(s) of a law, statute, or regulation
- The cause of a certain legal trend
- Why is a certain law, or regulation, necessary?
- The history of a law, regulation, or legal trend
- How are two laws or legal systems similar? How are they different?
- Whatever observation about the law, legal system, or actors you want to make!

Once you are done brainstorming, choose the final observation(s) that will serve as the topic of your research paper.

2) Gather your sources.

Head to the library, or log on to an online database, to find books, journal articles, newspaper articles, or research papers on the topic. If you want to make multiple observations, find a source for each of those observations. However, be careful not to overwhelm yourself by trying to find a source for *every* minute fact or statement you make. This step is mainly for finding sources for the **major observations** that are the purpose and backbone of your research paper.

Note that the source(s) may not support the observation by stating it, verbatim. Even if a source does not *exactly* state the same observation you want to make, it may still *support* your observation, so hold on to that source. For instance, it may give a similar opinion, provide context, or give some historical background about the subject. If so, you can use that source to add more dimension and analysis to your observation. Alternatively, the source may even contradict your observation or point you want to prove. Still hold on to it. Chapter 3, "The However Paragraph," shows how to use such contrary information to your advantage.

> Remember, if you get lost with finding sources, ask the librarian for help.

3) Read!

* Read the sources you have gathered with laser-beam eyes that are on a mission to detect sentences, graphs, opinions, and facts that support, or at least comment on, your observation.

* As you read, copy those sentences, graphs, opinions, etc. that are pertinent to your observation. Also be sure to write down the source name and page number (i.e., write the citation). Remember, this method is called the Observe ***and Cite***. Take note of the citation now, that way, you won't have to painstakingly go back and flip through all those books and journals, trying to find where a piece of information came from.

* Again, even if you come across information that disagrees with, or is the opposite of the point you are trying to prove, don't toss it out! You may be able to use that information in a "However Paragraph." (See Chapter 3, "The However Paragraph.")

4) Create a plan/working outline.

To avoid rambling away into the dark abyss of theory and superfluous words, create a writing plan. Professors can tell the difference between a well-thought-out final product and some random sentences mindlessly pieced together, and they are more likely to assign a better grade to the former. Below is a template to help get you started:

The Observe and Cite Structure:

I. Observation #1

* **Cite** to a source that supports, provides context, or disagrees with Observation #1
-Add commentary

***Cite** to a source that supports, provides context, or disagrees with Observation #1
-Add commentary

***Cite** to a source that supports, provides context, or disagrees with Observation #1
-Add commentary

II. Observation #2

***Cite** to a source that supports, provides context, or disagrees with Observation #2
-Add commentary

***Cite** to a source that supports, provides context, or disagrees with Observation #2
-Add commentary

Add as many observations (Roman numerals) as necessary to prove your point, or to meet the minimum word count or page limit. Also, for each observation add as many sources and commentaries (*asterisks) as necessary to explain and analyze your observation. Once your plan is completed, you are ready to begin writing your research paper.
Example plan/working outline of an Observe and Cite legal research paper:

SUBCONSCIOUS BIAS IN THE LEGAL SYSTEM

◇◇◇◇◇◇◇

1) Bias is real.

- Cite to source that supports, contextualizes, or even disagrees with my observation.
    - Comment on the content of the cited source.

2) Most people do not know that they are biased.

- Cite to source that supports, contextualizes, or even disagrees with my observation.
    - Comment on the content of the cited source.

3) Most U.S. judges hold some type of bias, be it racial, economic, or gender-based.

- Cite to source that supports, contextualizes, or even disagrees with my observation.
    - Comment on the content of the cited source.
- Cite to another source, etc. that supports, contextualizes, or even disagrees with my observation.
    - Comment on the content of the cited source.
- Cite to personal experience, or the experience of another
    - Comment.

> Yes, sometimes a person's (or people's) real experience(s) can be the "source" to which you cite. It is ok, if not preferred, to sometimes "switch up" the sources to which you cite

4) Bias affects U.S. laws, legal processes, and legal systems.

- Cite to source that supports, contextualizes, or even disagrees with my observation.
    - Comment on the content of the cited source.
- Cite to source that supports, contextualizes, or even disagrees with my observation.
    - Comment on the content of the cited source.
- Cite to source that supports, contextualizes, or even disagrees with my observation.
    - Comment on the content of the cited source.

Legal Research Papers: The Introduction and Conclusion

Please refer to Chapter 4: The Introduction, and Chapter 5: The Conclusion. The same principles contained in those chapters apply to the legal research paper.

Legal Research Papers: However Paragraphs

The However Paragraph is still pertinent to the law school research paper, as it is an advanced analytical move that shows you know different perspectives of the law. Refer to "Chapter 3: The However Paragraph," to guide you.

PART C

Tricks of the Trade

Use the following tips and tricks to add the final finesse to your university or law school paper.

Chapter 13

Help! I haven't reached the minimum word count.

So, you have finally reached the end of your writing assignment, and you've done everything you're supposed to do. You have:

Found the books, articles, interviews, and journals you need? *Check.*

Listed the quotes, facts, or research findings that answer your research question or otherwise jump out to you as interesting? *Check.*

Organized your research into a working outline? *Check.*

Completed your rough draft? *Check.*

An engaging introduction? A conclusion that summarizes? *Double check.*

"Ahhh, finally. All fini –"

Just as you're about to give yourself a pat on the back for completing your research paper, you realize you're just short of the minimum word or page count.

Whenever this happens, instead of allowing frustration to take over, just add more content to your paper using one of the following tricks:

Additional Commentary

- First off, can you add more commentary? Can you add your thoughts or experiences about a particular fact, or facts, you mentioned in your paper? Does a certain fact remind you of another fact? How does the opinion you mentioned interact with other opinions? If the above suggestions for additional commentary do not spark any ideas or get your writing juices flowing, no worries, try one of the following.

However paragraphs

- Have you considered *every* perspective of *every* fact and/or opinion mentioned in your paper? Chances are, you have not. So, use this opportunity to add another however paragraph (see Chapter 3).
    - If you become tired of starting a however paragraph with, "However," Chapter 3 provides suggestions for other ways to begin a however paragraph.
- After adding another However Paragraph, also add personal commentary to that new However Paragraph.
- Repeatedly add more However Paragraphs + personal commentary for other points in your paper until you reach the minimum word count or page requirement.

He Said – She Said

- My mom always cautioned against getting involved in gossip. She would warn us, "Don't get caught up in all that 'he said – she said' mess." In other words, she was instructing her children to stay away from the adolescent (and heck, even adult) drama that typically begins with, "He said you said I was ugly," or "Bill said he doesn't like you," or "She said you stink."

However, in terms of research papers and trying to reach the minimum length requirements, now is the time to pull out the "he said – she said." Except now, you are not repeating mean-spirited gossip that will break up friends or erupt into a fight, but you are repeating (and commenting on) what other researchers, authors, organizations, articles, etc., have said about the particular topic you are writing about, or something you mentioned in your essay.

- o So, when you're low on word count, go into "research gossip" mode. This may require you to do a bit more research, or review the sources you have already pulled. But start looking to find out what "he said" (i.e., an author, scientist, organization, perspective, etc.) and what "she said" (i.e., another author, scientist, an organization, or perspective).
- o Once you've found the "he said – she said" of a particular aspect, fact, or opinion of your paper, start adding to the "research gossip" by adding your own commentary to the goodies you have found.

<u>Add another section</u>

- Also, adding an entirely new section to your paper may work best for you.
  - o Perhaps while researching you came across another aspect, effect, or sub-topic. Now is the time to dig a little deeper into what you glanced across and see if there is any other commentary, articles, or books about that sub-topic.
    - For a Quote and Comment paper: Pull out other quotes, facts, or research findings that are tangentially related to the main topic of your paper, and comment on them. Before you know it, you will have added an entire page (or multiple) to your paper.
    - For an Observe and Cite paper: Perhaps there is an observation you have about the topic that you excluded, either because you thought it was irrelevant; you thought you wouldn't have space; or maybe you just had not had that "epiphany" moment until you began writing. If so, now is the time to tie in that extra observation, add your commentary, and get those last couple of words (or pages) you need to complete the writing assignment.

Chapter 14

Help! This doesn't sound smart.

I remember one time during my junior year at the University of Alabama when I had just finished a major writing assignment. Although I had completed the preliminary reading, formulated a superb working outline, and generated valid points, I was convinced that my rough draft still was not good enough. It didn't sound smart enough. After all, the book we had to read in order to complete the paper used these big, obscure words in every other sentence. So, as I constantly flipped to my dictionary to understand the obscure words that were being used, I took a mental note:

Ah. So this is what smartness sounds like. This is how I should write my response paper.

So, thinking I'd try something different and start to sound like a smart student, I turned up a notch the smartness volume on my paper.

In fact, perhaps I turned it up too much. One by one, I started swapping out boring words for their obscure, smarter-sounding, difficult-to-understand counterparts.

"Perfect," became "quintessential." (My fourth-grade language arts teacher taught me that one. She challenged us to use it on the state writing exam.)

"Name" became "moniker."

"Pictures" became "visual incarnations."

A few weeks later the professor handed back papers, and I was not happy with my grade.

"*B-?*" I thought in disgust. "*All that work and analysis. That was an A+ paper!*"

Then, I read his comments. It said something to the effect of: "You had the potential of great ideas, but I couldn't get past the use of obscure words being used unnecessarily."

A few lines down he circled in red "visual incarnations" and scribbled, "What is this?! Pictures? Images?"

Moral of the story: Although it is okay, and moreover *encouraged*, that you go back and revise your paper, do not go crazy with using "big" words. Here are some post-rough draft revision guidelines:

- **Choose clarity over sounding smart.**

First off, a well-written, smart-sounding paper is one where the ideas and points are clear, easy to understand, and well-organized. Contrary to popular belief, mindless rambling of random, high-level theories and conjectures will not automatically get you an A+. However, the instructor and/or professor will appreciate a well-planned, strategically organized assignment where the ideas, arguments, and points are clear and well-researched.

Secondly, what makes your writing "sound smart" is the content of your paper. The ideas you create, perspectives you present, opinions you critique, problems you analyze, and solutions you offer are what you should primarily focus on to make your paper "sound smart," not filling it with a bunch of words you don't really understand yourself. Adding too many big words that do not flow organically from your paper may lead to the big words distracting, and even frustrating, the reader.

- **Revise with a thesaurus. Swap out boring words for exciting words.**

Although you don't want to use obscure language like "visual incarnations" when you could have said "pictures," it is wise to revise your paper by adding a few fancy words in the place of boring ones. I know you're thinking, "But, Angel! You just said 'don't add too many big words!' What do you want us to do – use them or not?"

Do both. Note, I cautioned not to use ***too many*** big words that ***do not flow organically***. So, swapping out a dull word for a fancier-sounding word from a thesaurus is definitely encouraged, just make sure you don't do it for every sentence. As you read more higher-level texts and write more research papers, you will become better acclimated to know when you're going overboard. But for starters, do not refer to "pictures" as "visual incarnations."

I usually write and revise with the thesaurus on my computer open. Here are some common dull words, and their fancy, exciting counterparts that I prefer:

- o Things
- o issues, ideas, paradigms
- o factors, features, aspects, facets
- o entities,
- o aspects, devices, objects

- o Said (i.e., she said, this article said, that book said…)
- o offered
- o responded
- o critiqued
- o mentioned
- o According to X …
- o [Insert author's name] commented …
- o As referenced in X book…

- o Said (In narrative stories replace "said" by using a word that describes *how* the character said it.)
- o asked
- o answered
- o exclaimed
- o whispered
- o uttered
- o taunted

- **Fix choppy sentences.**

While writing your initial rough draft, you may slip into using the same sentence structure for every sentence. For example:

See Spot run. See Spot jump. See Spot hide.

As you revise your essay, vary the sentence structure, so that your writing does not sound choppy and bumpy, but instead flows eloquently. Change how each sentence starts by adding a complex, compound sentence here or there. Example:

> See Spot run. Also, take notice at how Spot effortlessly jumps on command and hides.

One technique to effortlessly switch up the rhythm of your writing is to add transition words and phrases. (See Chapter 15).

- **Proofread.**

Proofread! Proofread! Proofread! Once you're all done, go back and read your paper for spelling errors, missed words, or moments in the paper where you can explain something more clearly. Proofreading never gets old. It is a skill that was drilled into my head as an elementary student, and that skill was pertinent all through law school (and even currently).

Frankly, however, you will not catch every typo. Your brain knows what you intended to type because it knows the idea(s) you were trying to convey. As a result, it will automatically glaze over the misspelled word and give you a "pass." Hence, it is often beneficial to get a new pair of eyes to read over your work. Switch papers with a friend or classmate, where they proofread your paper, and you return the favor.

Chapter 15

Transition Words and Phrases

Transition words and phrases are necessary because they ensure that the ideas and arguments of your paper flow logically. They act as mile markers along your paper that signal to the reader where she is in your argument and what she should expect next.

Here are a few transitions to get you started.

First	Second	Third
First,	Second,	Third,
Firstly,	Secondly,	Also,
Primarily,	Next,	In addition,
First off,	Also,	Furthermore,
Most importantly,	In addition,	Further,
To begin,	Furthermore,	
To start,	Further,	

Last Idea	Concluding your paper	I've got more to say! (When you want to add another point and it doesn't fall within the "First, Second, Third structure)
Lastly,	In conclusion,	Also,
Finally,	To conclude,	Furthermore,
Also,	In summary,	Further,
Last of all,	Put succinctly,	Equally important,
	Ultimately,	Equally significant,
		Then again,
		In addition,
		Additionally,
		What's more,
		However,

I'VE GOT MORE TO SAY! (WHEN YOU WANT TO ADD ANOTHER POINT AND IT DOESN'T FALL WITHIN THE "FIRST, SECOND, THIRD STRUCTURE)	INTRODUCING AN EXAMPLE	INTRODUCING AN OPPOSING OPINION OR CONTRADICTORY FACT
Also,	For example,	On the other hand,
Furthermore,	For instance,	However,
Further,	Take, for instance, …	In contrast,
Equally important,	Case in point,	By contrast,
Equally significant,	For practical purposes, one can look to …	Conversely,
Then again,	X serves as an example of …	Alternatively,
In addition,	A practical effect of X is/would be …	Then again,
Additionally,		
What's more,		
However,		

CAUSE/EFFECT
Therefore,
As a result,
Hence, Consequently

Made in the USA
Monee, IL
08 November 2026

67969862R00083